To Matthew and Stephanie,
who have become the loving, kind and successful
adults most parents only get to dream of having.
I love you.

And to all
the women who have
the burning desire to move up
the *ladder of success:*

I am standing at the top of the ladder
with my hand extended to help you up
not kick you down

The type that appears as signatures on the baseball image on the cover of this book are fictitious and intended for creative expression only.

This book is a memoir kept in the form of a journal, not an autobiography. Every effort has been made to make this book as completely accurate as possible and is a compilation of stories told from my standpoint.

First Edition: November, 2012

Library of Congress Number 2012917408

ISBN#978-0-9858-197-0-5

Additional copies of this book available at:
www.playingballwiththebigboys

Cover designed by: Leslie Ann Shipley, Organic Idea Farm,

Author Photograph by Jennifer Orr Photography and Multimedia

Printed in the United States of America

317 E. 11th Street Chicago Heights, IL 60411

visit our website at: www.playingballwiththebigboys.com

About the Author

Debbie Halvorson was born and raised in a small suburb south of Chicago and grew up in a lower middle-class, blue-collar family watching her mom stretch a dollar while her dad worked two jobs. Debbie raised her children as a single mom and went back to college to get her Bachelor's and Master's Degrees while raising two teenagers and serving as Illinois state Senator.

She started her political career in 1993 as the first Democrat ever elected to the position of Clerk in Crete Township and went on to unseat a seventeen-year Republican Senate Leader--Aldo DeAngelis in 1996 the same year as a young upstart Barack Obama entered the state legislature. One of her proudest moments was passing a bill to lower prescription drug prices for senior citizens and people with disabilities. In 2005 Debbie became the first woman in Illinois history to serve as Senate Majority Leader. She learned that the rules of the game are as clear as mud and it takes more than honesty, loyalty and hard work to get ahead.

Debbie founded the Rosie Foundation, an organization to help women and children, because state and federal governments were cutting funds for social programs this segment of seciety desparately needed.

Debbie resides in Crete with her husband Jim Bush. They run two business together, share four adult children and five grandchildren. As President of Solutions Unlimited, LLC, she speaks and conducts workshops to teach women how to stand up for themselves, learn who they are and what their core values are so no matter what line of work they are in they can Play Ball With The Big Boys.

Do you want Debbie to speak to your group? Here is how to contact her.

visit her website at: www.debbiehalvorson.com or www.playingballwith-thebigboys or twitter: @dhalvorsonbush

or fb page: facebook.com/playingballwiththebigboys

Acknowledgments

We all live a very busy life and you could be doing anything right now, so I appreciate that you chose to read my book: Thank You. I have much gratitude for the many people who clarified and contributed so graciously to my stories and allowed me to make this book a success.

Thanks to my husband Jim for his love and support throughout this project. Thanks to my son Matthew and his graphic design skills and my daughter Stephanie for all the editing.To both of them for the creativity, generosity, loyalty and love that kept me going even when I wanted to throw this manuscript and five boxes of journals out the window. To my sister-in-law, Nancy Alex, and a great friend, Dr. Terri Winfree, who both labored long and hard to edit much of this work.

There is my other family: the Halvorson team. They worked for me while I served in Congress and are still there for me. Most contributed to this book whether by checking my facts, editing, choosing a title or telling me to keep going when I wasn't sure I could.

I learned so much from Lynne Klippell's online book writing class. The Write a Great Book class taught me more about writing a book than I ever thought possible. To me it was like getting a Master's Degree in Fine Arts. www.BusinessBuildingBooks.com

Regardless of the fact the following people were paid for their services they need to be mentioned because I believe in paying it forward. Special thanks to George Bogdanich for the extensive work done on this book with regards to his writing and research. Carl Johnson of Boyd Printing who printed the book, Leslie Ann Shipley of Organic Farm Ideas who designed the cover of my book, Jennifer Orr of Jennifer Orr Photography and Multi Media and Doyle Simms of Doyle Designed for doing my Headshot, Melanie Jongsma of LifeLines Publishing for some editing.

What Others Are Saying

"As a state Senator and a Congresswoman, Debbie Halvorson spent her fourteen years in elected office fighting for a strong middle class and serving as a role model to women across Illinois and our country. The first woman to serve as Majority Leader of the Illinois State Senate, Debbie shattered that glass ceiling through her tenacity as a legislator and her sharp political acumen. Playing Ball With The Big Boys draws on her astuteness and unique experiences in Springfield, in Washington, and in the heat of the debates that continue driving our politics today."

—Democrat Leader in Congress, Steny Hoyer

"If you think you have something more to contribute to your job, community, state or country, read this book. However, if you're waiting for others to take care of you, your family and career, don't. Debbie doesn't pull any punches or cherry-coat reality. If you want to contribute, be the best person you can be and get more out of life, step up and believe in yourself first."

Liz Weber —*Author of Don't Let 'Em Treat You Like A Girl: A Woman's Guide to Leadership Success.*

"American women are far from reaching their political potential and are excluded from most political power circles. Debbie Halvorson uses her experience to show women how to help each other become elected, gain power and to become effective in political office."

Kathy Groob, Founder ElectWomen and Author of *Pink Politics*

Engaging women in politics means one must demystify the politics and with this book Debbie Halvorson does just that. This book is a seamless integration of Debbie's personal story, political history, public policy and a career advice for women pursuing elected office. The conversational narrative lends warmth to the book and it's perfectly balanced by her candor about her experience serving in the 111th Congress. I was enthralled by Debbie's insider account of the hyper-partisanship strangling Congress and vitriol leveled at President Obama. At the same time I was inspired by her no nonsense practical advice for women pursuing office. She advises women to be intentional in their actions and above all to know and accept themselves. These words of wisdom would serve any woman well no matter her profession. Every woman in America has a stake in politics; every woman in America is touched by the decisions made in our governing bodies at every level. For the woman that wants to get off the sidelines and into the game reading this book is a great place to start.

—Kimberly Mitchem-Rasmussen, Executive Director of the Political Institute for Women

Debbie Halvorson is the kind of gutsy public servant who could give politicians a good name. Not surprisingly, her political memoir is an absorbing read, full of insightful back stories about herself and colleagues she's worked with, from President Barack Obama to her late Illinois Senate mentor Penny Severns. Every woman running for public office needs this book—it's an essential manual for success.

—Gloria Feldt, author of *No Excuses: 9 Ways Women Can Change How We Think About Power*

I am very blessed to have met Debbie when she was my Illinois Senator. I quickly realized how "real" she is and not just another politician. She befriended me, and has encouraged me to always strive to be more than I thought I could be and she is still there for me whenever I need her. I know through this book you will see how "real" she is and I hope you find the same inspiration from her that I have, no matter where your path may lead.

—Lori Gadbois, Kankakee County Recorder

Contents

Introduction

I grew up in a lower-middle class, blue-collar family, I raised babies, became a single mother with teenagers and served my neighbors as best I could.

There isn't anything I love more than my family and serving my community. I don't have all of the answers for what you may want out of life or public service, but I want to share my story in the event one small piece of it resonates and inspires you to overcome adversity and be the best possible person you can be.

I hope you don't read what I have to say as some kind of rule book. If you spent all your time trying to follow what I have to say you would have no time to be you. Everyone is different. That is why you need to create your own rulebook built from your own experiences and what works for you.

Each election is different, just as each state is different. Actually every level of government is different. What has become sad for this country; however, is the Republican districts are getting bluer and the Democrat districts are getting redder and the incumbents breeze along without much competition. All we are left with are extremes from both sides and it seems like the word compromise has become a bad thing.

Moderates are on their way to becoming extinct on both sides of the aisle and if you still happen to be one you better not tell anyone because you will be gone in your next primary. Don't get me wrong, there are yet places where general elections continue to pick their candidate and I am very grateful about that; however, more often than not it is in the primaries where candidates are being chosen.

Most people I talk to don't want to vote in primaries. Those who have heard me speak know that one of my favorite sayings is: "If you don't do politics, politics will be done to you." and it is happening every day. People are sickened by politics and politicians so they turn off the news, the debates and definitely those very expensive million dollar commercials. They vote in November for the same name that sounds vaguely familiar that they probably voted for last time. Nobody ever told them that they were supposed to be paying attention during their state's primary. God forbid you should have to go into a polling place and declare your party allegiance. You say, "it is none of their business, I will just wait to see who is on the ballot in November." Well guess what, you may not have a choice in November. You passed up that choice by letting politics get done to you.

I am hoping after you read even part of this book you will believe that you have no choice but to get involved even if it is just to vote in every election and gosh darn it declare one party or another if you have to; but make a decision the only place you have, even if it is in the primary.

There are countries that cancel their elections when they don't get eighty and ninety percent of the vote out. Why is it that we no longer care, that we are disillusioned, other than we have no confidence in our politicians. All the more reason to go vote or run yourself. That is another reason for my writing this book. I want you to realize that you don't have to be born into a political family or be wealthy to become a member of Congress. All you need is a passion to serve, priorities that fit your values and no personal agenda.

Because of my political experiences, I will be touching on women in political roles but what I have to say works for any form of leadership in any kind of work. There really isn't much difference except in politics you have to somewhat make people happy because you need their vote.

Men are making most of the decisions because they hold the majority of elected positions. Although women comprise half the US workforce and are the responsible decision-makers for the majority of consumer purchasing decisions, their median annual earnings are only around $24,000. Hillary Clinton mounted a powerful campaign for the presidency in 2010 yet in the end fell short of gaining the nomination, while the Republican ticket, with Sarah Palin as the vice presidential candidate, lost. The 2010 elections saw the number of women in the US Congress slip and the percentage of women in statewide executive positions decline to 22.4 percent from a high of 27.6 percent at the turn of the 21st century. It took more than 130 years for American women to gain the right to vote and it wasn't until 1933 that the United States saw its first female cabinet secretary. Countries like the United Kingdom and Germany have been led by women, yet the United States still hasn't seen a female vice president, let alone a president. However, so far no one I know wakes up in the morning and decides to run for office. Women need to be asked.

Another important part of my book that I don't spend much time talking about was keeping a journal all these years. I was able to write my book because I kept a journal. I want to encourage all of you to journal. Keeping a journal taught me who I was, what my priorities and core values were and how to stand up for myself. Journal writing is so beneficial not only to your emotional health but to your physical health. I don't get into journalling very deep in my book but I will have much more on my website. So I encourage you to sign up at www.playingballwiththebigboys.com for my secrets and lessons about journalling and so much more that didn't make it into the book.

Let me just finish with a bit on "confrontation" which I do mention quite a bit in my book. One of the main reasons that people fear confrontation is because they believe it is automatically going to get ugly. Women walk away from ugly, but please don't give away your power just to avoid discord. There is a belief that when you challenge someone the relationship will end up worse off than it was before. This is not necessarily true. If confrontation is handled properly it actually strengthens the relationship by opening up the lines of communication and removing obstacles. Women usually want to be liked by everyone which is another reason they avoid confrontation. Get over that right now. Your self worth is not determined by the approval of others.

So what is confrontation? It is the act of voicing a disagreement or discord, with the purpose of resolving the conflict, leaving the relationship between both parties in a new and better place. This isn't a fairy tale. Everyone can learn to handle conflict resolution in a way that actually leaves both parties better off.

So don't give up. There are always going to be days when you feel like your confidence is shaky and you are fighting a losing battle but remember to be consistent in your approach. People will grow to respect your consistency and you need to realize that it takes time to shape the patterns you have established.

1

A Call From the White House

Out of clutter, find simplicity. From discord, find harmony.
In the middle of difficulty, lies opportunity.
—Albert Einstein

"Hello Debbie, this is Barack."

As I was putting up Christmas decorations one wintry December day in 2010, the phone rang at our home in Crete, Illinois, a town thirty-five miles south of Chicago. I hesitated briefly before picking it up, knowing that any important call was more likely to go to my cell phone, but the voice on the other end was very official sounding. "This is the White House calling. Is Congresswoman Halvorson available?" "This is the congresswoman," I said, and the young lady went on to ask if I had a moment to speak to the President.

Even though he had kept us in session most of December and this was our only weekend home to get anything done, I was only a little surprised to hear the familiar voice: "Hello Debbie, this is Barack." Being on a first name basis with the President wasn't a lengthy journey, but it was a bumpy one.

Like many of my fellow freshmen congressional representatives who had been elected two years ago, I had just lost my reelection campaign the month before by a Tea Party-backed Republican candidate. Unlike the other first term members of congress, however, I had known Barack Obama since we were both elected to the Illinois state Senate fourteen years before in 1996. I had attended baby showers for his daughters Sasha and Malia. Michelle Obama had visited me in the hospital back in 2004 when I had a frightening scare with cervical cancer. Barack and I had both been taken under the wing of Illinois Senate President Emil Jones, Jr., from the outset of our careers and we had shared Dan Shomon, the very capable staffer that brought us both to unlikely victories.

While I was steadily rising to become the first woman to serve as Illinois Senate Majority Leader, Barack Obama was elected to the US Senate in 2004 before his historic run for the presidency four years later.

During the 2008 presidential election, I faced a difficult decision of whether to stay in the Illinois Senate in a position of power or listen to those who were urging me to run for Congress. The incumbent, Jerry Weller, had decided not to seek reelection.

It was true that Illinois government had reached a frustrating stalemate during the increasingly bizarre second term of Governor Rod Blagojevich and there appeared to be a good chance that Barack Obama would provide a fresh start in Washington after eight years of a Bush administration mired in two wars and a crushing recession. Of course, I had no idea that the US Attorney, Patrick Fitzgerald, would be setting up the arrest of Governor Blagojevich in his own home by the end of that year or the fact that two pieces of legislation I sponsored, would play a key role in Governor Blagojevich's demise. Nor was there any way for me to know that Illinois Senate President Emil Jones would announce his retirement. Had I known all these events would transpire, I don't think my decision would have been any different. I took Senator Durbin's advice to "never look back" on decisions made in politics. I am glad I made the decision I did to run for congress and wouldn't have changed a thing. Progress always involves risk. You can't steel second base if you keep your foot on first.

So that brings us back to the call to my home in the sleepy south suburban Chicago town from the President of the United States. That December day in 2010 was just a few short weeks after suffering my first political loss after what I felt had been a very productive term in office. I was at peace with myself as I spoke with the President. There was a little small talk and the President thanked me for my vote on the *Dream Act,* legislation that would enable children of illegal immigrants to attend school regardless of the status of their parents, and we talked about the miserably cold Chicago weather that he said he no longer missed.

I told him I was pretty sure he didn't call me to talk about the *Dream Act,* which had been defeated in the Senate, or the weather; so he moved to the real subject of his call. "So, Debbie, what do you think about the tax cuts?" This was the President's shorthand talk about the tentative deal with Republicans to allow all the Bush tax cuts to continue. It included the wealthiest segments of the population. He was also worried about crucial legislation that had been bottled up in the Senate by Republican leader Mitch McConnell. The Republicans refused to allow a bill to be called in the Senate to end the Bush tax cuts for those earning more than $1 million. This forced the president into a decision to continue across-the-board tax cuts that would also go to millionaires and billionaires—the alternative would be tax cuts for no one. Additionally, other vital legislation would be held hostage by Republicans in the remaining days of the lame duck session if the president did not agree to continue the Bush tax cuts for another two years.

I said bluntly that I was sick and tired of us always being asked to take care of these rich guys, though I understood his position. "You were Senate Majority Leader in Illinois," he said "you understand about compromise." All true; I pointed out, as I had on past occasions, that the Democrats' message was not clear or compelling, while Republican slogans against any tax hikes, even on the super wealthy who could easily afford to pay more of their share, were endlessly repeated and recycled especially through Fox News' outlets. The alternative facing the administration was to risk losing important legislation Republicans were holding hostage, including unemployment benefits, ending the armed forces' rule, Don't Ask Don't Tell, and the Start Treaty negotiated with Russia to reduce nuclear weapons. The President's frustration as he explained to me was getting our own Democrats on board with the tax cut bill to have a productive lame duck session. I told him even though I didn't like it, I would help him do whatever he needed because having been the Majority Leader in Illinois I understood compromise and getting things done. He said it would be helpful if he could add a quote from me in their press release and I said, "no problem." The call ended with a bit more small talk and I returned to my decorations.

Looking Back

Despite my lame duck status, I still had a vote on the upcoming tax cuts which would expire the end of the year. I had the sense that he was calling me in part to check the political pulse with someone he knew well and someone who would speak candidly from the perspective of a moderate Democrat from a Republican district. I had voted with the President on the *Patient Protection and Affordable Care Act, American Clean Energy and Security Act* (ACES) – better known as cap and trade energy legislation and *American Recovery and Reinvestment Act* (ARRA)—better known as the stimulus package. I disagreed with the President on parts of the financial reform bill but voted for the final version of the Dodd/Frank bill—to add regulations to the financial industry to prevent abuses like those that led to sub-prime mortgage failure and the economic meltdown of 2008. The compromise on the tax cuts that we discussed that day did in fact pass and led to passage of important bills in the lame duck days of the historic first session of congress in the new Obama administration, including an arms control treaty with Russia, legislation ending discrimination against gays in the armed services and a continuation of unemployment benefits.

Both of us knew there was a price to be paid for backing down from the Republican tactic of holding urgent services like unemployment checks hostage to Republican demands. Having succeeded in their legislative agenda by threatening to shut down some government services, would Republicans, fortified with a Tea Party dominated majority in the House be willing to shut down government if new demands were not met? Wouldn't they use this tactic when raising the debt ceiling came up in the new term?

Throughout his first two years President Obama showed repeatedly that his first instinct had been to compromise although sometimes to his own detriment. Many of us in the Democrat Caucus tried to tell him that the Republicans were never going to negotiate on the health care legislation. The Republicans never intended to support any part of the bill even when he thought he could win Republican support if he would drop the public option from the plan. All he did was lose considerable momentum during months of fruitless negotiations. Republicans never intended to vote for the health care legislation stalling as long as they could. Repeatedly, the president would endorse a Republican idea only to find them reversing their position and criticizing him.

The Republican opposition leaders he had to deal with were John Boehner in the House and Mitch McConnell in the Senate. They bore no resemblance to the responsible conservative Republican leaders of past decades like Everett Dirksen, Bob Dole or Bill Frist. In other words, Republicans with whom Democratic leaders could disagree, would still find common ground to pass urgent legislation. People who had been there a long time told me that when Tip O'Neill was the Speaker of the House, he and Minority Leader Bob Michel would fight all day long and then go out and have a drink together at night. Members from both sides of the aisle would socialize and even play golf together. Sadly, it seemed like civility has disappeared. With families living in their respective districts instead of Washington, no one takes the time to get to know each other socially anymore. There really isn't any time. Every spare moment is spent raising money.

Lucky for Me I Had a Supportive Spouse

Jim Bush and I were married in 2005 yet he had been a part of my life since I was a state Senator. It was enjoyable to Jim and I who no longer had children at home; we enjoyed being out every night going from one function to another together. I had already known Jim from his years of involvement with the Chicago Southland Chamber of Commerce. Jim grew up in Harvey, a Chicago Suburb. Unlike me, Jim did grow up in a political family. He learned at a very early age how to go door to door and had worked for quite a few politicians. The big difference between us was he was a Republican and I was a Democrat. While I was still in the Illinois Senate the differences in our party affiliation didn't matter as much since we set a few ground rules for our political relationship. He couldn't argue with my state politics and I wouldn't argue with his federal politics. Obviously, that changed when I went to Congress and he changed from being a Republican to being a *Debbiecrat*. When we got married his daughter Jill laughed and asked him, "Dad, does this mean you aren't a Republican anymore?" Jim's response is probably the same response many moderate Republicans have had over the years. He said, "Honey, I haven't left the Republicans, the Republicans left me. I am still right of center on most of the issues and it is a shame that they have forgotten people like me."

My husband Jim would drop me off at O'Hare Airport on Monday morning for either the seven or eight o'clock flight to DC, even though votes were not until evening. I would do some of my "call time" before I headed to my office for our weekly staff meetings. The time we spent raising money over at the Democratic Headquarters (about four blocks south of the Capitol) is what we referred to as our "call time". Some people called it their "happy time" but I found so many other ways to make me happy that I just stayed with the name it came with. Call time, one call after another to raise money. The TVs along the walls were always on so if votes were called everyone was off and running to the Capitol. Most representatives did call time. Some more than others. In fact at peak times when the room was packed you could hardly hear yourself talk.

The week was usually over on Thursday afternoons or Friday morning. The cars were strategically lined up outside the Capitol with assistants waiting behind the wheel. The members were packed and ready to go to the airport when votes were over. Reagan National Airport was close and if there wasn't any traffic (which you could never count on) we could get there in about fifteen minutes. Many of us would be on the same flight heading home for the weekend.

I had a very large district—Indiana State line on the east, one hundred sixty miles to the west into Bureau County, with a narrow strip of mostly farmland down I-39 to Bloomington/Normal. It looked like a capital letter "T". Counties included: Will, Kankakee, Grundy, Livingston, Woodford, Bureau, LaSalle and McLean. Jim and I spent the weekend traveling the district doing Congress on Your Corner events, festivals, parades, tours and whatever else we needed to fit into the short amount of time we were home during that particular weekend. Congress on Your Corner was a phrase coined by then Congressman Rahm Emanuel who felt you could go to a corner where there were people and have a meeting with a group of constituents. Over time they became organized events usually held in grocery stores, libraries or other places where the people were. Unfortunately, that is also the venue where Congresswoman Gabby Giffords was severely wounded, six were killed and thirteen others wounded.

I was a member of the Illinois Senate for twelve years (1997–2009) and as I said earlier, Barack Obama was also sworn in January, 1997. We certainly had our challenges moving legislation forward in the pay-to-play culture of Illinois but the hyper-partisanship we encountered in Washington after his election as President was of another order. While President Obama's victory in 2008 may have signaled that Americans were ready to accept an African American as President, there were still many for whom his election was an occasion for resentment and anger, an opportunity to go on the attack. The honeymoon that most new presidents might enjoy simply never happened and President Obama never got the respect he deserved. One doesn't have to like him or support him, but people should always respect the office. President Obama had been elected during the worst recession since the great depression, following the collapse of the sub-prime mortgage market and a string of failing banks and brokerage houses, including Bear Sterns, Lehman Brothers, Washington Mutual and Wachovia which happened in the last year of the Bush administration. Yet, you could hear daily broadcasts from conservative radio host, Rush Limbaugh, calling the economic downturn, "the Obama recession," even before he took his oath of office! As the Bush administration began moving out and the Obama administration moved in, Republican leaders increasingly took their cues from Limbaugh, Glen Beck, and others who fanned the flames with diatribes that had no facts. Much of this anti-Obama rhetoric came from the support of well-heeled corporate fundraisers like the Koch brothers who were the major funders of the Tea Party opposition.

Where is the Civility?

I cut my teeth on the rough and tumble life of Illinois politics, but nothing could have prepared me for the widespread acceptance of outright lies by opposition members who were prepared to believe the worst about anything connected to the Obama administration. Sara Palin's outrageously false claim that the health care bill would institute "death panels" had a huge affect in building opposition to the bill and influenced the public debate. Palin's repeated fabrication overshadowed many positive features of the health care reform bill that were widely supported by the public. Guarantees that insurance could not be denied for preexisting conditions, the removal of the "donut hole" to enable seniors to cover the cost of prescriptions and lifetime caps, financial relief for small businesses who could now pool their resources if they so chose and a requirement that health insurance companies cover young people until age twenty-six under their parents plan were facts that got in their way. If you were a small business with fewer than fifty employees the health care bill was not something that would hurt you instead would allow you opportunities.

While there was room for debate on different approaches to health care reform, Republican leaders failed to reign in their most vociferous followers who maintained a state of denial using ugly racial taunts and tactics. Tea Party activists in Washington, DC, spat on Black Congressional Caucus Chair, Emanuel Cleaver, as he walked into the Capitol. They called civil rights pioneer, Congressman John Lewis, a "nigger" and Congressman Barney Frank a "faggot." While Boehner and McConnell were silent over these outrages against their colleagues across the aisle, Michelle Bachmann simply denied to the media that the incidents even happened. At one point, a Republican colleague of mine from Illinois warned me that Tea Party activists were coming to picket my house in Crete. Tea Party enthusiasts such as Sharon Angle spoke ominously of "second amendment solutions" to policies they disagreed with. During this time I often ran into US Representative Gabrielle Gifford, who shared her worries over the mounting hostility she was experiencing at home, particularly on immigration issues. Gabby and I were part of a group of half a dozen members of Congress who lived in the same apartment building. We would sometimes meet on the roof of our building at the end of a long day to talk about issues and people we encountered. The fears that Gabby expressed would come back in a rush to all of us in 2011 when we learned on a horrifying Saturday morning in January during a routine "Congress on Your Corner" meeting that she had been shot and grievously wounded by a deranged gunman in Tucson, who also killed US District Judge John Roll and four others. I must admit there were times during meetings I held around my district that I felt I was in danger of being shot or killed myself even though people can't legally carry a concealed gun in Illinois. One person told me on social media that I better have more than one gun because I was going to need them. I didn't have time to dwell about it, I had a job to do. However, these are the things that bothered my husband, Jim, immensely. I am proud to say that although I am a strong and independent woman it is nice to know chivalry is not dead. Jim was bothered because he felt helpless; whether watching me endure the lack of civility by people who came to see me during my Congress on Your Corners, or whether it was to read the lies said about my colleagues and myself on the Internet [that he took very personally] or when it was being cornered at events. People like Jim want to fight the good fight but only when both sides believe in fighting fair. Men like Jim are about fixing things but in this caustic atmosphere it wasn't about fixing America, it was about dividing America.

As Tea Party threats mounted against members of Congress over the health reform bill in the late summer of 2009, US Representative John Lewis of Georgia sought to put things into perspective in a caucus meeting: "We must stand on courage," he said, "and not worry about the threats that we are receiving. We should worry about the people who may not have health care if we don't get this bill passed." The message was welcomed by Democrats in the caucus, but the Capitol Hill police and the FBI were not taking any chances, as they stepped up their efforts to assure the safety of any member who felt threatened.

As excited as I was to become a member of Congress, I quickly saw that the election of President Obama in 2008 had changed the political dynamics on Capitol Hill. The election had mobilized a well-organized opposition during the lame duck months of the Bush administration that was already in place when the new President and new session of congress began. This opposition was not at all interested in compromise, but was strongly dedicated instead to making President Obama a one-term president and ready to deprive him of any legislative victories, no matter how the country suffered. The word compromise had become a four letter word.

My Soapbox or Maybe My Pet Peeve

The approval rating of congress is at an abysmal nine percent and voter turnout is at an all time low. Moderates on both sides of the aisle are about to become extinct. There is nothing but gridlock in Washington, DC, because no one wants to even mention the word "negotiate" for fear they will be the next primary casualty. So what does all this mean? Out of the 435 congressional districts maybe fifty are still competitive in a general election. The rest are solidly Democrat or Republican. Red (Republican) districts are becoming redder because if a Republican doesn't tow the conservative line, that member will most definitely have a primary challenge. The same is true in the Blue (Democrat) districts. The redder and bluer the districts are becoming just means that the extremes in each party are electing their nominees. My unscientific research has shown that it is still difficult to get the majority of the electorate to vote in primaries for a number of reasons. So what does that mean to the average person? It is sad but simple. A very small amount of extreme voters are electing the people who represent you in congress. But do the elected people really represent you? Probably not. However, until people start getting involved in the process by voting in their primaries, instead of getting angry and tuning everything out, nothing will change and Democrats will continue to elect the extreme left and Republicans will elect the extreme right and the two shall never talk, negotiate or meet in the middle because the people who elected them DON'T WANT THEM TO. Negotiation and compromise have become bad words. God forbid they are caught talking to someone of the other party. Someone gets wind of it and before you know it, that person has a primary challenge and its all over. Okay, so I am being just a little facetious, but not much. It happens.

I ran into this woman who approached me about term limits. She said, "Term limits would fix all of our problems. Throw the "bums" out . They stay too long." It hit a nerve I didn't know I had. In concept getting new blood is good and every election there is still that option to get rid of a bad elected official. In the past my answer to term limits has been sort of generic. I told her "If we are automatically getting rid of legislators, good and bad, what is to stop lobbyists and staff from making all the decisions? Once you get rid of the legislator, the staff doesn't go too. The staff member now goes on to the next legislator who is brand new and has no idea what is going on. That person will now rely on the staff members who are the only ones with the institutional knowledge and will be running that office." She was dumbfounded. She thought the staff person should go too. But, the nerve I found that I didn't know I had, was that she wanted term limits to do *her* job. She said just get rid of these lying, cheating, no good. . . . I don't need to finish all the things she said. I asked her why it shouldn't be the responsibility of the voter to get rid of the elected official? She said to me "Probably more than a five minute conversation huh?" I am no longer in elected office so I won't be in a position to vote for or against term limits anytime soon, but if I am ever found to be in that kind of position again, let me say right here: I am more against term limits now than ever. Term limits? To make voters like this woman who stopped me to say she was for them because they would make her life easier so she doesn't have to bother taking the time to vote? Not a chance!

Bill Clinton Was Not Very Popular With the Right

Some forget the depth of hatred the right wing had for Bill Clinton—many people wondered where that came from. He was the first president who had come of age during the Vietnam War and active in the antiwar movement. He also beat George H. W. Bush who was seen as carrying on President Ronald Reagan's legacy. Most Republicans just despised him because he won. By the end of his first term Clinton found the formula to beat the Republican lock on the White House, but not until he took his own shellacking during the midterms in 1994. Clinton was able to come back with a vengeance in 1996 and although there were quite a few bumps in the road personally and professionally, somehow the former president has become one of the most popular Democrats in our history. The Republicans started going after Clinton his first day in office just as they have President Obama. During Clinton's administration the Republicans conducted thirty-seven different investigations meant to destroy him politically. Most of these were investigations conducted by the Judiciary Committee and there was nothing the Democrats could do about it. So even though some think Obama was the first president who has gone through such disrespect, it has happened before.

No Stranger to Hard Work

I had a reputation in Springfield as a hard worker; often being at the office around six or seven o'clock in the morning to be available to the other members of the caucus. Senate President Emil Jones wanted me to handle all the new members of the Senate who were elected in 2002 and there were many due to redistricting. Going from the minority to a super majority was a good problem to have but it also meant that everyone wanted to pass their entire agenda immediately. Having the votes to pass any bill you wanted did not mean you could get the other Democrats automatically on board and the new members did not understand why. They soon learned they needed to ask the other Democrats for their vote and were not happy when the answer wasn't always yes. A large number of the Democrat caucus had never been in the minority before. My job was to make sure everyone had their questions answered and understood what was going on since freshmen were discouraged from talking in the full caucus. I made a point of being well prepared. When people asked why I worked the long hours year after year, I said, "It's not work, if you love what you're doing."

Once in Congress the poisonous atmosphere created by Obama's more extreme critics, made the work much more challenging.

There were many factors that had led me to forgo a safe seat in the Illinois state Senate. I had many strong connections in Washington, including the friend I expected to become the new president and I was convinced, that even as a freshman, I would be able to help my congressional district a great deal. I had a very good relationship with Senator Dick Durbin, the powerful Majority Whip. I also had a good relationship with Rahm Emanuel, whose relentless energy and single-minded focus helped Democrats restore their majority in the House of Representatives in 2006 and later became President Obama's choice for Chief of Staff. Rahm had a big part in recruiting me. In fact he talked to my husband, Jim, before he talked to me. Jim happened to be in DC for a chamber of commerce event and Representatives Schakowsky and Emanuel teamed up on him to tell him about all the reasons I should run. The reason that made Jim laugh was when Rahm said we would see the world because of all the travel you do as a member of Congress. Jim told him that obviously Rahm had no idea what this eight county district looked like with all the parades and festivals, that there would be no time for travel other than inside the Eleventh District. Rahm called him a neanderthal and assumed he didn't want his wife to better herself. Jim definitely set Rahm straight that he was NO neanderthal and made sure the Congressman knew that he supported his wife 1000%.

2

Where It All Began

What lies before us and what lies behind us are small matters compared to what lies within us. And when we bring what is within out into the world, miracles happen.
—Henry David Thoreau

I was born in March of 1958, during a time of racial upheaval. I would like to say I was from a family of activists that immediately instilled the value of social justice upon birth, but we were just a regular family that lived a quiet, hard working life. The most important thing to my mom and dad was family.

My great-grandfather, Alphonso DeFrancesco (we called him Pa) and his family emigrated to this country from Italy to work at the Steger Piano Factory in a town that was originally called Columbia Heights. Pa transitioned from the old country and laid down roots.

John Valentine Steger opened a piano factory in 1893 on twenty acres of land alongside the railroad. The railroad town also boasted a second factory, a general store, a post office and a burgeoning housing stock. With 324 residents, the village incorporated in 1896. John Steger agreed to pay $400 toward election costs if the name of the town was Steger rather than Columbia Heights. Steger won and Columbia Heights was no more.

John Steger played an instrumental role in the town's development. Along with the piano factory, Steger planned a residential subdivision. Learning from the mistakes of George Pullman, he encouraged home ownership and independent commercial development. Serving two terms as village president, Steger oversaw development of a volunteer fire department, water and sewer facilities and a unique system of underground pipes which provided steam heat for workers' homes from the heating plant of the factories. He also recruited German craftsmen, developed assembly-line manufacturing of pianos and designed special rail cars for shipping them. By 1920, Steger was the "piano capital of the world," producing more than a hundred a day. Phonographs were also manufactured there.

John Steger engaged with the industrial leaders of Chicago, joining the Union League Club and served on bank boards. In 1910 the Steger Building was completed at the corner of Jackson and Wabash in the Loop as his administrative and display center for the pianos. Designed by Benjamin Howard Marshall, this nineteen-story structure still stands.

After Steger's death in 1916, the factories continued until closing in 1926. Having depended on one major manufacturer, the village was particularly vulnerable during the Great Depression. However, the remarkable collection of buildings continued to be a key employment center. In 1930 a macaroni factory started in one of the old buildings and several years later local craftsmen joined together to manufacture radio cabinets in another. At its height of activity the Steger Furniture Company employed close to 700. Following other uses over time and a major fire the buildings were demolished in 1972–73. By the end of the century, a small strip commercial area, a large Kmart and a huge expanse of asphalt parking lot covered the site which is what it looks like to this day.

My Family

My dad went into the Air Force by the time he was eighteen and was stationed at Bentwaters Parks Base in Woodbridge, Suffolk, England, where he met my mom Joyce Miller. They got married in January of 1956 when she was only seventeen. Head over heels in love, she left her mom, six brothers and sisters and her motherland to come to America to start a life with my dad and his family. My mother didn't waste any time learning about American ways by the time I was born in 1958. My brother Richard, Jr., came along a couple of years later so it seemed we all learned about the country together. When I was just seven my parents allowed my brother and me to take the day off school to go to Chicago and watch my mom become a US citizen. Even then I knew how proud I was of being an American who was living in the type of place that valued people of all backgrounds and talents. I was raised in a place where you were proud of an honest day's work and that anything was possible if you were willing to work hard enough for it.

My grandfather, Tony DeFrancesco, (we called him Papa) continued in the family craftsman tradition and worked at City Furniture refinishing and repairing furniture. My grandfather was short in stature and wore a fedora like most Italians, especially during his generation. When I was young and he would visit there was a special place on the table next to his chair that he carefully placed his hat and no one touched my grandfather's fedora. He liked his coffee a special way and he knew if it had been sitting in the pot to long, but would never say anything except to leave it in his cup when he left. That must have been where my dad and I got our taste for a perfect cup of coffee.

My parents worked tirelessly from as early as I can remember; my dad was a produce manager at the local Kroger grocery store and my mom held down the fort at home. When Kroger closed and my dad lost his job he and my grandfather decided to go into business together and started Suburban Furniture Repair and Refinishing. They rented a small store front on the main street in Steger, hung out their "shingle" and decided to continue in the craftsman family tradition. The two of them were artists; they loved what they did and were also good at it. If part of an ornate chair leg was missing they would custom carve a new one and stain the wood to match perfectly. Their craft was the true definition of a family business where my mom learned how to cane the seats of chairs by hand and us kids regularly visited what we called *the shop*. Customers loved my dad and my grandfather and they loved their customers right back. Even my children, Stephanie and Matthew have fond memories of visiting *the shop* and listening to customers tell my dad stories of their antiques and the many miles the furniture had traveled just to continue to be part of their daily life. Thanks to Suburban Furniture Repair, family heirlooms live on today, still beautiful and functional to be passed on to future generations.

My grandfather died in 1983 from lung cancer. To me it seemed like we found out one day he had lung cancer and he was gone the next. All I know is it wouldn't have mattered how much time the doctors had given him, it wouldn't have been enough time to prepare for his untimely death. I was very close to my grandfather and still think of him often.

My dad decided to continue the business alone. The work my dad and grandfather did was labor intensive so my dad was now dealing with twice the work and half the manpower. There was never enough hours in the day and he was already working nights and Saturdays but now he was working Sundays. It was my brother Richard who told my dad one Sunday morning that if my dad wasn't going to church, neither was he. That was probably the last Sunday he went to work at least during the time church was going on. After church we ate a typical English dinner with a roast, potatoes, vegetables and Yorkshire pudding. The roast was always large enough to make meals for most of the week.

It never occurred to my dad that the hours and this kind of work was taking a toll on his health. Being self-employed, obtaining affordable health insurance was next to impossible. My mother was a magician the way she could make a dollar stretch but there still wasn't enough for insurance costs. It was nothing short of a crisis when at the young age of forty-nine my mom was diagnosed with breast cancer. It was difficult to watch as they fought the bills instead of being able to concentrate on fighting the illness. Thank God, after chemotherapy, several different wigs and developing a strong resolve to survive, my mom made it not only past that magic five-year mark but is alive still today. We prayed for good health every single day for the next fifteen years until she could get health insurance again, which came in the form of Medicare.

No one in my family was particularly political but they appreciated their community, regularly voted, and were civic minded. When I was a little girl I loved walking down the street with them on Election Day to watch them vote. The polling place was in the basement of a neighbor's house. The only thing I remembered was a lot of food and good conversation. I loved hanging around listening to their stories and I laughed right along with them even though I had no idea what anyone was talking about. I don't remember debating politics and policy around our dinner table but I do remember watching Bozo on the day when news broke that President Kennedy had been shot and my mom started crying.

I am the oldest of three children and the only girl. I consider myself lucky to have grown up in a rough and tumble neighborhood with mostly boys. I learned early on that I needed to keep up, have a thick skin and not cry under any circumstances. Summer days meant we would leave the house in the morning and come home when we heard the sirens go off at nine o'clock at night.

My brother Richard was very smart and was often picked on for being a "geek". He wore husky pants with a pocket protector and in July of 1969 when he was ten years old, he decided he was going to be an astronaut. That was when he sat glued to the only television set we had as Neil Armstrong become the first man to step foot on the moon. Richard stayed true to his dreams graduating from University of Illinois as an aeronautical engineer. Wearing glasses had prevented him from becoming an astronaut. I remember being his protector, willingly getting into fights with anyone to ensure he wasn't hurt. I wore my hair in braids because I was tired of getting it pulled by the neighbor boys. I realize now it was their way of getting my attention which of course did nothing but make me angry. This is one of my first memories of not backing down from confrontation.

My grandmother owned a resort in the Ozarks. It was called Singing Hills Resort. During the summer my cousins and I would take turns spending a few weeks at a time with her as long as we didn't mind cleaning the cottages and doing chores every morning. I loved being able to greet the new families especially those with kids and I knew I could make an extra buck or two by hanging around the fisherman and offering to clean the fish they caught. At night, I was able to carry around a pocket of quarters for anyone who had trouble with the pin ball machines. At twelve years old it was my first taste of being in a leadership position and making sure things went smoothly at the Clubhouse.

That was the first twelve years of my life: running around the neighborhood, playing baseball, fighting with neighborhood boys so my brother could read his science books in peace, visiting with my family members, eating mayonnaise sandwiches on white Wonder bread and spending two or three weeks each summer in the Ozarks and camping with my own family. Then we all were in for a pleasant surprise when my youngest brother Michael was born.

At twelve I was happy to have another boy around to play protector to, but by the time I was sixteen I wasn't sure I still enjoyed playing with a now four year old. I wanted freedom, not a little passenger; but that was the deal if I wanted the car. One day I took Michael with me to my friend Joyce Paape's house to help them get ready for a big party they were having. Mrs. Paape loved making jello salads and already made four of them, leaving them to solidify in what she figured was a safe, mischief-free refrigerator. She was always so quiet and couldn't say anything loud if she tried; but on this day all I heard was a very loud, "oh no". We went running to see if everything was all right. She was okay, but her pans of jell-O sure weren't. Michael had put his grubby toddler fingers in each pan of jell-O and as he was licking each finger he wasn't sure why we were all yelling at him.

Of course I could forget about a high school romance when there was an entire period where my boyfriend at the time had to pay Michael a quarter every date we went on just to keep him out of the way. Michael was the best chaperone my parents could ever imagine. Michael grew up to be a wonderful adult and I don't think he sticks his fingers in jell-O anymore but he will give you the shirt off his back if you need it and he knows more about electronics than I ever will. I don't have to do research when buying anything new, I just call Michael. When he isn't off helping someone chop down a tree or recover lost files on their computer, he is working on heavy equipment somewhere as a member of the International Union of Operating Engineers.

My sometimes nosy, baby brother wasn't the only thing that distracted me from being a love-sick high school student. At Bloom Township High School in Chicago Heights, Illinois I was officially bit by the public service bug even though I was painfully shy. I know everyone has awkward adolescent teenage years, but I felt so out of place and uncomfortable in my own skin, I would rather sit in my room, alone, surrounded by my radio and books. My challenge was figuring out how to get past my shyness to get involved in government.

Vacations—Even During the Oil Embargo

My parents had a small trailer that was pulled behind their car. We did a lot of camping during the summer. Our favorite places to go were Cadillac, Michigan and Monticello, Indiana. I believe the first time we took a trip and stayed in a hotel was to Disney World in Orlando. It was 1973, I was in high school, my little brother Michael was in preschool and it seemed like it took forever to get there. Gas averaged only thirty-six cents a gallon but it was during the oil embargo and gasoline was rationed. We passed many gas stations with signs saying they were out of gas and when we did get to a gas station with gas we were not allowed to fill up usually only able to get ten gallons.

School and My First Taste of Political Office

I was a diligent student that always did what was asked of me and often ahead of the due date. So freshman year during the requisite speech class I had to overcome what I could only consider the trauma of public speaking. I had written my speech but could not physically bring myself to get up in front of the class to give it. The teacher thought if she threatened me with an "F" that I would reluctantly get out of my seat. I stood rigidly in front of her without the ability to form words and took the failing grade. As I've referenced previously, I come from a long line of hard workers and this type of grade was not to be tolerated in our house.

It was incredibly challenging, but it was that "F" that put me on a path I would have never have dreamed of. I started getting involved in activities that pulled me out of my comfort zone and gave me a growing sense of self-confidence.

At the end of my Junior year, I ran for secretary of the senior class (and won). It is probably hard to believe but our class had almost 2,000 Bloom students and getting to know everyone was not easy.

Vocational education was very popular when I was in high school. There were all kinds of programs like 4H, Future Farmers of America, Distributive Education and the Office Education Association (OEA) which is the program I applied to be in. I was accepted into this program because of the other office and business electives I had chosen. OEA was one of those classes where you received school credit for getting a job based on your class curriculum. I worked in the main office of my school at the switchboard making two dollars an hour. My OEA cohorts and I competed in things like typing, job interview skills and public speaking on the local, regional, state and national level.

It was Mrs. Pressendo, the OEA advisor, who taught me what running for office was all about. For OEA, we held class elections and I was surprised to find myself elected president. On the regional level I ran and won the office of vice president. Mrs. Pressendo and I were practicing for the national competition that was coming up in Topeka, Kansas, when I became enamored with public service and using elected office to make a difference. Bloom Township High School had never held one of the coveted national offices. Elections were done by weighted vote based on number of students enrolled per state and the largest amounts of students represented high schools from states like Ohio and Texas. I had finally cultivated enough courage and confidence to run for office even though we knew it would be a long shot. This was the first time I stepped out of my comfort zone in a very big way. We had a point to prove. It takes confidence, something we had built in this class. Mrs. Pressendo and the OEA gang helped develop a much-needed gimmick in order to have any chance to win this kind of election. By the time the convention rolled around we were ready. Everyone was in costume and our song was golden. We were Snow White and the Seven Dwarfs and our rallying song went like this:

Hi ho, hi ho, vote Debbie DeFrancesco
She'll work for you, the whole day through
Hi ho, hi ho.

Now come on, if you had to listen to this song for four days and see us in the halls everywhere you went, who would you vote for? I won as a regional vice president, and became the first national officer Bloom Township High School ever had and the only one we knew of from Illinois in a very long time. I guess, in retrospect, I was on my way to serving in public office and didn't even know it.

Off to College

Upon completion of high school, I went to Robert Morris College (RMC) in Carthage Illinois to get my Secretarial Degree. I had heard so many good things about RMC but my biggest decision was figuring out whether to commute to the Chicago Campus or go four and a half hours away to Carthage. Once I figured out how I would borrow the money the decision was made: I would go away for the whole college experience.

No one in my family had ever attended college and I really hadn't thought much about it during high school. Back then, Junior and Senior year of high school didn't revolve around guidance counselor appointments, faraway college visits and colorful University pennants stapled to my bedroom wall. Instead, this was a time where I was expected to get married and have a houseful of babies. Why waste the money on a four-year degree that I couldn't afford?

Carthage was 265 miles away from Steger and the farthest I had ever ventured from home for an extended period of time. I immediately threw myself into the grueling coursework of speed typing, shorthand and message taking. I look back on my first venture into higher education and laugh at the courses I took so seriously. I had no idea how quickly the business world would change and evolve with new technology. I felt the skills from these ancient classes were going to be the best way to prepare myself for the real world—my real world of being a wife, keeping up a house, raising babies and perhaps temping at an office here and there to supplement family income.

The courses were important to me, but like many poor college students I needed a job. I became a Resident Assistant of my dorm and a tour guide. I not only needed the extra money, I wanted to do something where I could connect with people and feel like I could make a difference in people's lives. Comforting them during the dreaded high school to college transition, being an ambassador to a school I felt so comfortable at and letting the students know when the ONE payphone per floor was available for the next caller, kept me really busy. One of the jobs I did as an RA that I never expected to do was take a young girl to get an abortion. I was glad to be available for her because she didn't know where to turn. It was her first time away from home and she had no idea how her boyfriend's protection failed. We talked for many weeks about how she was feeling and what was going on with her not only physically but emotionally. She tried to tell her parents and couldn't. The only decision for her was an abortion. I took her across the wobbly Keokuk, Iowa, bridge one morning to sit with her while she had her procedure. I get very angry when people talk about decisions such as this being just a simple trip to the health center. These are agonizing decisions and not something done lightly. It was a very quiet drive back to the dorm and I stayed with her until she was ready to talk about her experience. To this day I have never broke the promise I made to her back in 1977 of never telling anyone of where the two of us went and why and unless *she* shared that experience with anyone, the two of us and the people at the Health Center are the only ones any wiser.

This was a big turning point in my life that taught me so much about trust and being trust worthy and what it means to be a real friend. I could have told her I disagreed with what she was going to do or I could have gossiped about her to others but I didn't. We all have opinions and we all want to express them but they are just that: opinions. Because of this experience I believe that no one, especially the government should ever force their beliefs on another and am therefore pro-choice. Each situation is different and no one should judge. I believe in Roe Vs Wade because that supreme court case is not about abortion, it is about the right to privacy. It is that right to privacy that everyone deserves.

Whatever free time I had left I traveled extensively. My freshman year of college was also the year I served my term as a national officer of the Office Education Association. I went to exotic faraway lands like Michigan, Indiana, New York and Ohio. We wore our green blazers with ribbons and big name badges and boy did we feel like big shots. If I was afraid, I didn't show it. I was used to not showing my emotions. I learned that early in my life. We spoke in front of other elected officials on other levels and represented the Office Education Association (OEA) at conferences where all the different organizations attended like FFA, DE and 4H.

The Real World was Waiting

My secretarial degree from RMC took ten months to earn. I graduated and like almost everyone else, commuted into Chicago for work. I excitedly took the *Metra* train each day with the thousands of other commuters. My first job was in the John Hancock Building working at an advertising agency. At this point, it was the 1980s, but my life wasn't a Robert Palmer or Madonna video. The world I lived in wasn't filled with bright neon Ray Bans and over sized off the shoulder sweatshirts. My fellow commuters and I inhabited a world of sensible greys and pinstripes. Our three-piece brown suits for the men, over sized shoulder pads, big hair and tennis shoes over our pantyhose for the women. We all made the mad dash off the train and down the street scurrying to slave over a typewriter.

I had several jobs all of similar responsibilities. The one that stood out the most was an opportunity to work for the Office Education Association's national headquarters: the organization I had just spent a year traveling with. They wanted me to move to Columbus, Ohio and work at their national headquarters as Administrative Assistant/Receptionist. It was a small office and we were the ones who coordinated all the conferences.

I was filled with bittersweet emotions; one fleeting second I was sad about the prospect of leaving my hometown and my Italian family I was so attached to. I had just come home after being away for a year and was finally settling in to a nice routine. Two hundred and sixty-five miles away in Carthage, Illinois was one thing, but Columbus, Ohio, was so far away, it might as well have been another planet. The next second I was excited about being a young woman ready to take on the world even if I did only have a college secretarial certificate.

In the end, the idea of a new adventure won. I was nineteen and still terrified to disappoint my parents or go against their desires and expectations. This was among my first memories of becoming the master of my own destiny, being the captain of my own ship in control of making my own life. Explaining this once in a lifetime opportunity was one of the hardest conversations I had ever had with my parents. They were staunchly opposed to my moving away and I brought up how my mom left England when she was only seventeen. It is tough for parents to argue once a precedent has been set and I took the job sight unseen without even having a place to live or knowing anyone in Columbus. Those were easy details to figure out once I got there. My mother suffered with debilitating migraines her entire life and had been taken unexpectedly to Mayo Clinic a couple of weeks before I was to start my new job in Ohio.

So the weekend before I was to be in Ohio, a friend and I drove to Mayo Clinic in Minnesota to check on my mother. It was strange being in that hospital room, knowing I was about to officially start my life as an independent woman. My dad must have also sensed the magnitude of the moment and it was the first time in my nineteen years I had ever seen him cry.

I had to report to work that following Monday and couldn't put my departure off any longer. I made the trek home from Minnesota, picked up my tiny U-Haul carrying all of my earthly possessions and then went on to make the six-hour drive to Columbus, Ohio.

During one of the conventions I was working at, I met Gordy Halvorson the man who would be my future husband. He was four years older than me and part of the OEA Alumni group who also held their events in conjunction with ours. He would help me get all my work done so I had time to go out for dinner with him on occasion. I naturally found this helpfulness very charming.

After about a year, the National Safety Council stole me away and I was back in Chicago to work. I taught classes like Bicycle Safety and Defensive Driving to instructors who then went out to teach students. I traveled extensively with this job also.

It was while I worked for the National Safety Council that my long distance relationship with Gordy became more serious. Long distance relationships are not very practical. He and I talked on the phone every night and I received some kind of card or letter in the mail every day. We took turns traveling back and forth on a couple of weekends a month.

Marriage

After about eight months of courtship, he proposed. I never did ask, but I don't think the proposal was planned. We were at a Minnesota Twins/Kansas City Royals baseball game and started discussing whether or not I would be moving to Minnesota. I happened to tell Gordy that my dad said I couldn't move again until I got married. So without even thinking, he proposed.

We were engaged for a year because we still needed to figure out the logistics of our life. Where to live, where to work. He was a farm boy from Minnesota and loved where he lived. I was tethered to Illinois and my family in the Chicago suburbs. I wish I could remember the conversation of where to settle down because it was the type of issue that can make or break a new partnership. Eventually Gordy got a job in Illinois making almost twice what he made in Minneapolis so that was an easy way to break a stalemate.

I was a practical girl with a compulsory need to make realistic decisions. I had no desire for a large wedding. I wanted to get on with the life I had mapped out for myself of marriage and housekeeping and babies. My mother being a traditional woman from England was excited to mark the occasion with a big celebration. Most of her family from England were attending and she coordinated most of the details of the big day herself.

We rented a little five hundred square foot, two-bedroom place next door to my parent's house. Rent was only $125 a month and in 1979, interest rates were at a whopping eighteen percent. Certificates of Deposits (CDs) fetched fourteen percent interest and we were able to save quite a bit of money for a down payment on a house. Working, living close to my family, adopting an adorable collie/golden retriever mutt named Bear: Gordy and I were living the American dream.

Children

On October 31, 1981, we had our first child Stephanie. When I entered the hospital all the nurses where screaming that I just couldn't have a baby on Halloween and I told them to be quiet because it was only noon, she was not waiting until tomorrow. First children are always perfect; Stephanie slept through the night by the time she was a month old, never cried unless she needed something, and she walked at nine months old because I had something in my hand she wanted and just couldn't wait for me to give it to her (she was stubborn). She read fluently before she went to school because she was tired of others reading to her when she knew she would like the books better if she could read them herself (I told you she was stubborn).

The little five hundred square foot house we lived in seemed to shrink once Stephanie was born. Her nursery was situated on the side of the house that faced my parent's dining room and she would wake up to the sight of them having morning coffee and cookies. She would bounce in her crib and smile seeing the familiar faces of her grandparents just fifty feet away. While I loved this proximity to my family, I knew it was time to move. If you opened up the playpen in the living room, there was only room for one person and they had to stand. We finally bit the bullet in 1982 when Stephanie was eleven months old and bought an 1800 square foot, brick house in nearby Crete. The owner sold us our house on a five-year balloon contract for twelve percent. Compared to eighteen percent interest, we figured we did pretty well. I always wanted children and staying home with them was fine with me. I was twenty-three years old when I had Stephanie and had just turned twenty-six when Matthew was born. Stephanie was so happy to get a new little baby brother to hug or should I say choke. Every picture we took of the two of them she is holding him so tight the whole world knew how much she loved him. Judging by his size no one worried about Matthew being able to take care of himself. He was born weighing more than eight pounds compared to Stephanie's six. In fact by the time Matthew was one, he wore a size four but to his credit he did wear them for a couple of years. In contrast to the daughter who slept through the night by one month Matt didn't sleep through the night until he was two years old and he had a head full of blond curls that I just couldn't cut and Stephanie had very little thin, blond hair. The two of them looked like twins and I only made it worse by dressing them in those cute boy and girl look alike outfits. Our days were full of Sesame Street, reading books, taking walks in the neighborhood and going to the park; any activity that was going to cost little to nothing.

Before we got married Gordy and I had discussed that he would be the breadwinner and I would quit my job once we had children. I was happy to agree. Gordy was twenty-seven and he was ecstatic that he was already exceeding his goal of always earning an income that matched his age. Gordy was a computer programmer—a rare skill in 1981—and was very good at it. Making $30,000/year was a huge accomplishment for him and I was proud to support him.

I was pregnant when I started selling Mary Kay Cosmetics and once Stephanie was born I would be quitting the job I had running an apartment complex. Mary Kay was something I could sell because of the flexibility and repeat sales. I did very well and continued selling until I became a Senator in 1997 when it became apparent that my customers would suffer from a lack of attention.

Before the children started school, I became involved with the Crete Women's Club. It worked out well for me because there was a babysitter on site for those of us with small children. It enabled me to do things with and for the community and the women who lived in it. I was very young and the majority of the women in this club had been members for many years. I was in awe of them and what they had accomplished and soon I was engaging with them in groups such as the Great Decisions Discussion Group where we talked about topics such as foreign policy, the environment and promoting democracy.

Once the children began school, I was available to go on field trips, be room mom, computer mom or whatever it was the teacher needed. Several times during the week it was me you would see in the hallway doing math problems with the kids or helping them on the computer. I can admit it now but it was the first graders that were teaching me how to use the computer instead of the other way around.

Stephanie was very active in gymnastics before she went to kindergarten and was on the gymnastics team by third grade which started the three and four hour practices almost every day of the week. She loved it and was so good. Today I watch my six year-old granddaughter Ellie during her gymnastic classes. Things haven't changed much. Ellie was glued to the 2012 Summer Olympics and Gabby Douglas, just like Stephanie did with Mary Lou Retton during the 1984 Summer Olympics. She was a Bulldog cheerleader, member of the girl scouts and played the violin.

Matthew tried his hand at baseball, tennis and wrestling but it was his football story that still makes me chuckle. I think he was in third grade and after one of the games he told me that he couldn't take it anymore and begged me not to make him go back. I really didn't want him to quit midway through the season but I let him continue his story. He said he needed to get out of there or they were going to *kill* him. He was so convincing I figured that was enough for me and that was the end of Matt's football career. The years he played the Bass it was bigger than he was but that was the instrument he picked. Matthew was also a cub scout. We still have the trophies from all those Pinewood Derby cars he had to carve out of wood. The story that he is proudest of, or should I say activity was when he and a friend got the crazy idea to streak across the football field during the Homecoming game his Senior year. He told me he wanted something to remember about high school. He sure accomplished that. In fact, he even made America's Funniest Home videos.

Work/Campaigns/Running for Office Myself

A good friend of mine, Jeff Sopko has a Farmers Insurance office. While out socially one evening, he mentioned he needed someone in his office to do his bookwork part time. I worked a few hours a day while the kids were in school. It was perfect and then in 1992 Jeff decided to run for the Will County Board and asked if I knew anything about being a campaign manager. I said "Of course I did" and that was the start of our long campaign relationship together. There was no time to lose and we got busy knocking on doors, raising money and sending out mail so everyone in Eastern Will County knew that there would be a Democrat on the ballot that could win which had never happened in District One before. Once we had some money I told Jeff we needed to get signs printed since the election was right around the corner. We took a picture of him, went to a local printer and had signs made up on yellow card stock. We purchased yardsticks and stapled the newly printed posters with Jeff's picture onto the yardsticks and that weekend brought in all the volunteers and put the signs into the ground. The bright yellow could be seen for miles (well almost). Little did I know it would snow the next day and once yellow card stock got wet, it fell off the yard sticks and all the volunteers who had just been out putting those signs together and out were not too happy with me. Jeff called me and said, "I thought you knew how to run campaigns?" I did, we just hadn't done signs in our campaign. So we started all over again, but this time we ordered them through a professional sign company. We received them just in time for the election. We got our volunteers together again, put out the signs and the night of the election, with hundreds of supporters together at a local restaurant, we watched Jeff win as the votes trickled in late into the night.

Jeff Sopko was elected to one of three seats on the Will County Board. After that election, Jeff knew that there must be a few Democrats in the Township and decided to put a Democrat slate together for the 1993 spring Crete Township elections. I had no intention on being one of the slated members because I had really caught on to this campaign manager stuff. But I did end up running for clerk.

The following Spring, we shocked everyone when three of the Democrats on our slate won. A year and a half later was the 1994 Republican landslide elections when it seemed like every Democrat that was on a ballot lost. Silly me, I decided to walk into my office the morning after the election while all the Republicans were sitting around gloating and one of our Trustees said to me, "What are you doing here? Didn't you go down with the rest of the Democrats?" I just looked at him with a smile and said under my breath of course I didn't and walked into my office because I had work to do. I was not going to lower myself to their level. There had never been a Democrat elected clerk in Crete Township before and they thought I was just a fluke.

Before the 1993 elections, the sitting board had not had any opposition so they voted themselves huge raises, health care and Illinois Municipal Retirement Fund (IMRF) Pension benefits because they thought they could do anything they wanted. They did not realize that they would be called on the carpet because of it. It didn't take long but our Democrat colleague Andy Qunell didn't like being in the minority and decided to run in the next election as a Republican.

I had run for my first office because I believed that elected officials were supposed to serve the public and all I saw from the Township Officials in Crete before us were a group of people who never had opposition taking care of themselves. After I was elected I established our Town Hall office as a satellite office to the Will County Clerk so that our constituents no longer had to drive the thirty miles to Joliet to get a marriage license, birth or death certificate. Having lived in the Eastern most section of Will County my entire life, I knew my fellow constituents would welcome this convenience. What confused me is why it took so long to provide services to the people. Could it be that when you have no opposition, there is no mandate for change?

3

Obama and My Parallel Paths

The greater danger for most of us is not that our aim is too high and we miss it, but that it is too low and we reach it.
—Michaelangelo

Township Clerk to the State Legislature

Unlike Barack Obama, who already had a long term game plan when he ran for the Illinois state Senate in 1996, I had to be persuaded to run for the legislature that year against powerful Assistant Majority Leader Senator Aldo DeAngelis, a Republican. Apparently, the fact that I had been elected clerk of the Township of Crete as a Democrat in a very Republican district was noticed by two of the state's most powerful political leaders; Mike Madigan, Speaker of the House and Emil Jones, Minority Leader of the Senate. They were both looking for someone who had a chance to defeat Republicans who represented the mix of suburban and blue collar towns in the South Suburbs of Chicago.

Being a clerk was one thing but running for the state Senate was a much steeper challenge and I had my doubts whether this was the right move for me. I had two children eleven and thirteen and a husband whose behavior was becoming increasingly erratic and was somewhat opposed to my running for higher office. While Obama had attended Harvard Law School, I had only a secretarial certificate from Robert Morris College. Senator Emil Jones, who had worked as a Chicago sewer inspector and first served as a precinct captain when John F. Kennedy ran for President in 1960, was very persuasive.

I was attending a reception for township officials when I first met Senator Jones. According to Emil's staffer Dan Shomon, Emil had seen me meeting and greeting people "working the room" as he called it, and was impressed. I had sold Mary Kay cosmetics for a number of years and it had become second nature for me to connect with people. Jones took me aside at the party and said: "Debbie you would be a perfect candidate to run against Aldo DeAngelis" (the incumbent senator of nineteen years). I looked at him like he was crazy. No one ever ran against Aldo.

Incumbent Senator Aldo DeAngelis

He was bigger than life itself. He was elected in 1979, the son of an Italian immigrant steelworker and graduated from Bloom HS as I did. He had a great sense of humor and was congenial and direct. There was no mistaking the headfull of silvery white hair that many say made him look like a typical senator. As I was staring into space thinking of Aldo, Emil brought me back to earth and said, "I know you would be great because we have been looking for someone who is energetic, young, female and a Democrat from the Republican part of the district. A moderate Democrat could take over this seat. The only thing that would make you *more* perfect would be if you were Italian." I just started laughing and said, "I am not sure I want to tell you this, but my maiden name is DeFrancesco." Senator Jones brightened and said, "Perfect, that settles it. You are our candidate." I smiled and told him "thanks but no thanks," but Emil Jones kept calling me six or seven times in the following days positive he could change my mind.

At the same time Senator Jones was pursuing me, so was Tom Cullen of Speaker Madigan's staff. Ironically, Lori Joyce who was on Jones' staff was dating Tom Cullen. There was quite a bit of tension between the two of them because they both had orders to recruit me. Finally, they decided it would just be easier to keep my name off limits in their discussions of daily activities. I began my homework on the two offices, the people who currently held the office, the challenges that needed to be overcome, the size of the districts and concluded that although it would be more difficult to run for senator than representative, I would take on the bigger of the two challenges and ran for senator. Luckily it didn't hurt Tom and Lori's relationship; they eventually married.

Despite the initial hesitation, once I decided to challenge Senator DeAngelis it was going to be an all out effort. By election day I had walked all 210 precincts, going door to door. Along the way I developed a very strong sense of what concerned the voters. If no one was home when I dropped by I wrote a note on my campaign literature: "Sorry I missed you." Early on in my campaigning I skipped homes that had an Aldo DeAngelis yard sign, but on a few occasions someone would come running out of the house to ask for literature and wanted to hear what I had to say as a candidate. They explained that they were forced to put up DeAngelis signs in their yard but it didn't mean they would be voting for him any longer. Even then, before a string of scandals rocked Springfield, there was widespread public perception that the Illinois government was for sale and that strong reform legislation was needed.

Relishing his role as incumbent, Aldo DeAngelis could be very arrogant and he had a bit of the bully in him. When we spoke on one occasion he basically patted me on the head, a patronizing gesture I didn't appreciate. During the campaign he showed his displeasure when I attended some of the public events he had hoped to monopolize. "What are you doing here?" he would ask with a sneer.

Thereafter, when the Republican controlled Crete Township Board cut my salary in half they tried to make it look like it was job related and fed the information to Aldo to use in his campaign speeches against me like it was my own fault that my salary was cut and that this somehow proved that I was not ready to be a senator. Meanwhile, our campaign developed a tight organization of volunteers with no frills. The campaign headquarters was in a warehouse whose owners later tried to turned it into a strip club after our campaign was over and started building things like the "stage" before election day so it made for quite a conversation piece.

Getting Help from Then (Somewhat) Unknown Barack Obama

Senator Jones called me at one point to tell me that a young attorney and former community organizer named Barack Obama from Hyde Park would be helping my campaign because he had no opposition of his own. Obama had taken care of that by successfully challenging the bogus signatures collected by three other candidates seeking to be on the ballot including Alice Palmer, a one time Obama mentor who had decided to run in the Congressional special election in 1995 that Jesse Jackson, Jr., won.

Alice Palmer had encouraged Barack Obama to run for her seat, but once she lost to Jesse Jackson, Jr., she expected Obama to step aside, so she could run for her old Senate seat again. Obama had already put together an organization and was ready to begin his political path as a state senator. Alice Palmer was well liked and respected, but she had run a poor campaign in the special election for Congress and the signatures did not meet the election specifications to be on the state ballot. Some of Obama's Hyde Park political friends never quite forgave him for knocking Alice Palmer off the ballot, but other observers saw it as a sign he was serious about politics, willing to play hardball.

Since Obama had no opposition, he offered to help in other campaigns, so I dropped by the small civil rights law office where he worked and he wrote me a check for a campaign contribution. Barack gave the impression of a friendly, but very serious young man whose ambition was evident from the start. He promised to come down and campaign for me, and he did so several weeks later.

Obama Walked Precincts for Me

He brought with him a smart young political operative named Will Burns who eventually went to work for Emil Jones, then became a state Representative and is now a Chicago Alderman. Dan Shomon, who Emil Jones had wisely assigned to run my campaign, greeted Obama and three well dressed volunteers from Hyde Park upon their arrival at the campaign headquarters. He sent them with a map and literature to walk door to door in the upper middle-class African American neighborhood of South Holland. When Barack returned with his volunteers, he expressed some surprise that the neighborhood had already been visited by the campaign recently.

"Yes, we were there last week and the week before," Shomon replied, "and the week before that." Obama quickly realized that Dan and the rest of the campaign were very thorough and left nothing to chance. He must have been impressed enough with Dan that after both of us were elected to the state Senate and Shomon was assigned to me as a staffer, Obama asked Minority Leader Emil Jones if Dan could work for him. Jones objected to Shomon working for Obama saying he would have his hands full working for me because everyone knew that I would be the number one target by the Republicans in 1998 and Dan Shomon already knew my district. Shomon also opposed the arrangement at first, telling Jones his impression of Obama was that he "wanted to change the world in five minutes" and he "didn't have time for that." Shomon had a long dinner with Obama and was won over to the point that he would help guide Obama through the thickets of the Illinois General Assembly and up the political ladder under the watchful eye of Emil Jones. So it turned out that even though Shomon had his hands full with my candidacy, he would be staffing both of us.

My Mentor, United States Senator Paul Simon

At the time, I had no idea what lay ahead for Barack Obama, but my campaign brought me in close contact with a man I had long admired, US Senator Paul Simon. I had read Paul Simon's books both as source of inspiration and for his insight into the political process. Paul Simon chose not to run for reelection in 1996, but he walked precincts in my district with Michael Giglio and myself. Michael was the candidate running for state Rep in the northern part of my Senate seat. Michael was married to Lisa and they own Calumet City Plumbing. Michael's dad, Frank Giglio, was Thornton Township Democratic Committeeman so their veins were full of political blood but somehow I think Michael was not as big of a fan of the political scene as his dad was. Paul Simon had a distinguished career as a lieutenant governor, congressman and US Senator deeply committed to reform, decency and progressive politics. As a young newspaper publisher in

Madison County, in Southern Illinois, he bravely exposed extensive corruption in local governments, which led to his being called to testify on the subject before the US Senator Kefauver's Special Senate Committee investigating corruption in the 1950's. I knew that those members of the Illinois legislature who sponsor ethics legislation in Illinois face a daunting and often lonely task in the pay-to-play culture of Illinois, that often seemed reform resistant, but I also knew I would have important allies. A number of them stood with me the night I defeated DeAngelis by twelve percentage points, and they included the Illinois Coalition for Political Reform which had a film crew led by the capable Jim Kales, on hand to record my victory.

Talking about Michael Giglio reminded me of a funny story. We spent much of our time knocking door-to-door. It is truly the only way to win elections and connect with the people. Michael and I had it down to a science as to the routine and as we approached a door that was Michael's turn to do the talking, a nice old lady came to the door with her little dog that would not stop barking. I knew we were going to have a problem when Michael just rolled his eyes and said, "Great, just my luck." Try as he might, the little old lady couldn't hear a word Giglio was saying. Finally through his frustration he just stopped and the lady must have felt bad for him and said, "I am so sorry" and Mike decided to let it go and said, "that's ok" and she looked up at him and said with a funny look on her face, "I was talking to my dog." That was it, Mike Giglio stormed off pledging never to knock on another door ever again.

It was Dick Durbin who was running to replace US Senator Paul Simon in 1996 who we would see everywhere on the campaign trail. It wasn't until after the election when Senator Durbin and myself both won that Durbin admitted to how bad he felt for me on the campaign stump. He loves telling the story now that everywhere he went he would see this young energetic young lady who was everywhere campaigning her heart out. He would ask the person he was with, "Didn't anyone tell her she couldn't win?" Well she did win. That should be a lesson to everyone who runs. Keep your nose to the grindstone, work like heck and do the job necessary all the way to election day. You too, can win. Look at Debbie DeFrancesco Halvorson, no one ever thought she could win. But she did.

Barack Obama and I Are Both Sworn in as State Senators in January, 1997

Sometime after the election, Aldo DeAngelis' campaign manager said the reason I defeated the incumbent senator was because "Aldo knew all the bank presidents, but Debbie knew all the bank tellers." That was certainly part of it. I also better identified with people of modest means because that's how I grew up. Kristen McQueary who covered the legislature, wrote in a magazine article: "Halvorson, of Crete, is known for her bubbly personality, which makes her an anomaly among a stodgy group of Senators." Rich Miller of *Capitol Fax* called me a "Pollyanna" in my early days. So, I continued to smile and focused on learning the ropes especially when it came to constituent services and to see what I could achieve at a time when Democrats were in the minority in the Senate. Being in the majority and having control meant everything. We also had an aloof Republican Governor in Jim Edgar who was not going to share any credit with Democrats. Even if I were not a freshman senator, the Republican committee chairmen would make sure that any legislation sponsored by a Democrat would not get out of committee. The party in control decides who gets what passed and when. If you were Debbie Halvorson in 1997 serving in the minority,who only had a two year term and who most people believed got elected because of a fluke anyway, you were not going to get much accomplished. I suppose that is why one of my colleagues bought me a mug that had the words "boys I'm taking charge here" on it. The words were stacked on top of each other and if you took the first letter of each word, it is probably what they really wanted to call me.

Poker Anyone?

The newly elected state senators—myself, Barack Obama and Terry Link, who represented Lake County north of Chicago, were placed in the least desirable offices, adjoining each other, so we saw one another often in the course of our duties. It was Terry Link who later organized the poker games that enabled Obama to bond with legislators on both sides of the aisle. The rules were that no politics would be discussed during the course of these games, which allowed the players to get to know each on a friendly convivial basis. While Obama was learning the game he often lost money. Senator Link and Senator Larry Walsh who were Obama's seat mates were two who often benefitted from Obama's losses and they would joke that they hated to see Obama move on because to them "It was like having a second job." Whatever Obama lost on cards, however, he more than made up by making connections that would help his meteoric rise through the ranks. Senator Larry Walsh was from Will County and arrived in Springfield a few months after the three of us because of an appointment. Larry and Barack as well as Terry became and have stayed very close friends over the years.

I didn't play poker, (good thing, because I didn't have to complain they didn't let girls in) but I quickly made friends with the overwhelmingly male members of the Senate. Having grown up with brothers it was easy enough for me to be "one of the guys." Aside from my fellow freshmen, Obama and Link, I made friends with many Senators early on such as Pat Welch, Jim DeLeo, Larry Walsh and Bobby Molaro. Senators Lisa Madigan, Bobby Molaro and myself went to the movies in the evenings instead of the restaurants and bars along with friends Rich, Jeff and Jay. The one thing that still makes me chuckle was thinking about how the guys would argue about where to sit in the theater. Whether it would be in the front row or the back row, on an aisle or in the middle; Lisa and I would just laugh while we watched these guys try to make a decision. We didn't mind where we sat. After a few movies we figured it was easier to go our separate ways. When it was over we laughed and talked about our favorite parts of the movie and went home.

Initially eager not to stick out, I kept my hair short and wore pant suits. How crazy of me to think no one would notice I was a girl, but I wasn't going to let the fact that I was a female be noticed before my talents and abilities, which is what I preach today and what is repeated among other great points in Liz Weber's book, *Don't Let Em Treat You Like A Girl*. I went to the extreme as if to say you can't look good and be smart at the same time. What I stress now is to watch that fine line and make sure you don't cross over into a place where your femininity is the only thing people see first because many in the workforce will never get to see the talent and skills you possess. It would be several years before I felt comfortable wearing more feminine attire.

It did bother me, however, when I attended functions, checked in at the front desk, gave my name and they would ask "What Senator are you here to represent?" and I would respond that I was the Senator. I am glad things have changed and we have many younger senators, male and female and those kind of things don't happen as often.

Even Senators Have to Start out as Freshman

Freshmen were under the very watchful eye of Emil Jones, and poor Dan Shomon gained the nickname as my shadow. Senator Vince DeMuzio loved to joke, laugh and ask me where my shadow was. With my own strong feelings about ethical dealings and as a sponsor of ethics reform legislation I didn't really need a chaperone, but I understood and appreciated that Leader Jones was trying to protect me from doing anything that the Republicans would use against me in the next election. As a freshman in the minority from a marginally Republican district, I was the biggest target for defeat in 1998. Two years? I know I was under the impression that all terms for senators were four years; but they are not. All senators run three times in ten years. This just happen to be the two-year term. As a result, I didn't get many bills passed and I understood that from my first day so I worked on perfecting things within my control like my constituent services. I didn't spend as much time in the beginning spinning my wheels trying to sponsor legislation that wasn't going anywhere. I would just add my name as a cosponsor and worked with the Republicans to pass a bill I normally would have sponsored myself. When bills I sponsored did reach committee, key Republican senators sought to humiliate me if they could by allowing me to testify and then voting the piece of legislation down solid no matter how uncontroversial. These were the kind of lessons that taught me more than what I learned reading the 'how to' manuals. I became a better legislator; although so much more could have gotten done if this kind of system didn't obstruct progress.

Hit and Run Bill—Very Personal to Me

I was quite determined to have one bill in particular pass no matter the obstacles placed in my path. It was a measure that would make it a felony to leave the scene of an accident when someone is seriously injured or killed. This was very personal to me because of a situation in Crete where a motorist hit and killed three of five young children who were walking along a dark road and sped off. Instead of reporting the accident he checked himself into a hospital so he could sober up. When he was finally arrested the prosecutors not only had to prove that the driver knew an accident had occurred but that it involved another person instead of an animal or object. I worked with the families of these young sixth graders to craft a bill to address hit and run drivers. Senator Bev Fawell, Chairman of the Transportation Committee did everything in her power to stop it. She explained that it wouldn't be fair to the person who committed the crime, not to be able to reach his or her attorney before reporting the accident. I wasn't thinking about anyone needing an attorney, I was thinking about saving someone's life. Eventually, between the families, my persistence and the TV coverage we were able to generate on this story, a compromise bill was reached with Senator Fawell and it passed overwhelmingly.

Women's Groups

I attended a training session for new legislators through a group called Women in Government. This is a nonpartisan group that is made up of women legislators on the state level that provides leadership opportunities, forums and educational resources to address and resolve complex policy issues. Being new I found these sessions quite helpful when dealing with the issues in the legislature and I became very active with them, eventually serving on their Board of Directors and many task forces.

Illinois also had a great group called COWL (Coalition of Women Legislators). Each year it was lead by two legislators; a senator and a house member one Democrat and one Republican. I may be a bit biased but Republican Representative Patti Bellock and myself made such a great team, we led COWL for two years. During our years, Patti Bellock and I worked with an organization headed by Debbie Walsh of Rutgers University—Center for American Women and Politics (CAWP) to help young women get started in politics by holding a weeklong program at the University of Illinois in Chicago. The senators and representatives volunteered their time as mentors and we actually lived in the dorms with the girls. It was so successful and something I would like to see duplicated if funding was readily available.

Dreams from My Father

Barack asked Dan Shomon to arrange a book signing for his recently published book: *Dreams From My Father: A Story of Race and Inheritance* and I was more than happy to join a small group of seven or eight senators at the Springfield library. It was an enjoyable event, but Barack Obama was still unknown to the public at the time and the book sales reflected that. Some months later when I saw quite a few copies of *Dreams* on the bargain table at a Springfield bookstore, I bought them all. Barack graciously signed my books and I gave them out to all my friends and family. How could any of us have known that this book would suddenly become a bestseller more than ten years later when Obama, now a national figure, began to reach the peak of his popularity during his campaign for President? When I finally found some time to read his book I thought it was remarkable for its candor about his white, Kansas-born mother and the African father he barely knew, but whose unrealized dreams cast a powerful shadow over a young boy growing up in Indonesia and Hawaii and making his way to Columbia University and Harvard Law School. It was the work of a young man still finding his identity, and it offered a lot of personal insight into the forces that shaped him and his outlook about a country still grappling with racial issues.

Learning the Leadership Ropes

Minority Leader Jones was instrumental in helping us both, teaching us the ropes in ways that promoted our political careers each in a different way. My interests were not my own personal agenda but with helping our Democratic Caucus grow; I rose through the leadership positions quickly as Jones valued my honest and trustworthy behavior. I was appointed to my first leadership position just two years after arriving in Springfield. Whenever we would get together outside of Springfield and Jones would announce he needed money for a fundraiser or candidates in an upcoming election, I was the first one to write a check while many of the others in leadership complained about parting with their money. I spent much of my leadership years chairing the Democrat Caucus before moving on to Assistant Majority Leader and eventually making history as the first woman to serve in Illinois as Majority Leader. Keeping control of a group that all had opinions and felt they needed to talk first could be difficult at times but eventually we all got along. Freshmen were never encouraged to speak, they were told to listen. This rule was somewhat tongue in cheek but most fell for it. Not Obama; he spoke in caucus as a freshman all the time but as someone who knew the constitution as well as he did, it was encouraged and the majority of the other senators listened to what he had to say and on occasion even asked a question or two.

Obama, on the other hand had no interest in leadership within the caucus or if he did, it was not made known. His desires were clear he wanted to ascend the political ladder and received help from Jones in passing bills that would have been difficult for a relatively new senator to pass without help from leadership. When Obama began referring to Jones as "my political godfather," we decided to have some fun with that. I changed the ringtones on Leader Jones' cell phone to play the theme from the "The Godfather." It's still on his phone to this day, I believe.

The Balancing Act of Work and Family—Never Easy

To me, balance means fifty/fifty. You would be hard pressed to find any woman who could honestly say she spends fifty percent of her time at work and fifty percent of her time at home. In my case, it wouldn't have mattered if I was spending 100 percent of my time on my home life. Home life had become a nightmare. Gordy's drinking sessions became a marathon and I could never predict when he might erupt at home. While I was away in Springfield (doing my job as senator), I would get calls from the kids that he never arrived home. Thank God for my parents who were around to take care of them when necessary. Throughout my life I have always been in a position to help others especially the problems faced by women and mothers. Yet, at home, like a lot of women, I was hesitant to stand up for myself. Sometimes we think we are doing the right thing by staying married even if it is just for show which is what I was doing while raising my children on my own. I thought I was doing the right thing for my children by playing that kind of charade. Our children are smarter than we are and much more resilient. The children seemed to understand sooner than I did that the abuse was not going to go away. In one fit of anger, Gordy threw a television at me on election night because I wanted to see my vote totals. Fortunately it missed but Gordy kept taunting me: "You will never leave me. You'll never get a divorce. You can't take the publicity. The newspapers will have a field day." I tried everything to make things work. I even booked a Disney Cruise for the four of us and a few days before the cruise Gordy tried to set the vacation documents on fire in front of both kids. Nice guy huh? I was able to salvage the paperwork but not the cruise. It was a disaster and when Stephanie, my insightful daughter of only fifteen, called me a hypocrite for helping others but not myself, I knew I had to do something.

Double Standard?

Emil Jones learned that there were problems in my marriage, though I suspect he did not know how serious they were. He was adamant, however, that I should "stay married, keep smiling and act as if everything was fine." I was so offended even though I am sure Emil meant well and was trying to protect my political career, but there was a double standard at work that bothered me. I did not believe that my male colleagues would be given similar advice and the extent of the abuse I was experiencing could no longer be tolerated.

Couldn't Take it Any Longer

Finally, things reached the point of no return when my daughter Stephanie came home from school early one Friday afternoon and saw Gordy with his hands around my neck threatening me. Stephanie had the presence of mind to calmly go upstairs and call the police. The police made Gordy leave and that was the last time he was in our house. Thereafter, whatever sense of decency he once had seemed to have died. I don't know what happened but he quit his job and lived off of the money he made from the equity in our house and whatever retirement he dipped into. Little did I know what struggles we had ahead of us, but as Stephanie and Matthew learned it is adversity and the struggles you go through that teach us about character.

I had been dealing with our children's needs on my own anyway and we would find a way to manage following the divorce. Ever since the children were in grade school I had taught my children the value of a dollar. At the end of summer vacation each year I would give them each $100 and it was up to them to figure out how to make sensible choices on a limited budget regarding school clothes. They complained of course, but they learned to live within a budget. Emotionally, it wasn't an easy time for me. When I first became a senator, I cried half the way to Springfield. My son was in junior high at the time and I would take him to lunch, take him back to school and drive to Springfield. I'd be thinking: Am I doing the right thing? I was doing the right thing. It stopped me from being a smothering mother and it allowed them to become the successful wonderful young people they are today.

Getting My Bachelor's and Master's Degrees—Not Easy

During my time in the state Senate I went back to school to get both my Bachelor's and Master's Degrees at Governors State University. I always wanted to go back to school anyway and figured this was as good a time as any with Stephanie going away to the University of Illinois and Matthew ended up going to the same University two years later. When most were going out and having fun in their spare time, I was doing homework. When you go back to school when you are forty-one you have a completely different perspective—B's were not tolerated. Luckily Matthew and Jim didn't mind being my test subjects and it really didn't hurt them to learn so much about communication and training anyway. I was chosen to be the class speaker at graduation which gave me a chance to publicly share my degree with them. I remember filling out three Free Application for Federal Student Aid (FAFSA) forms each year that took hours to do and each year we would receive word that no one in the family qualified for anything. I was a single mom with a salary around $50,000 and all three of us were in college at the same time. I understood there were families with much more need than me. Because of my situation I was empathetic to the needs of families, especially single moms with more than one child in college who received no financial help. During my time in the state Senate there was a program available to us that allowed me to award eight one-year (or two four-year) scholarships/waivers to students in my district going to Illinois universities to be given out at our discretion. It was a program that all state legislators enjoyed but a luxury that should have been eliminated long ago because of those who abused the system. In many cases without that first year of college help they may not have ever gone on to get a college degree so I was happy to help. I did not hand my waivers/scholarships out to campaign donors or friends. I appointed a committee each year that chose the recipients from applications submitted to me. Some of the criteria I asked my committee to consider were things such as what I went through with multiple siblings in college, what they wanted to do with their life, ability to pay, grades etc.

I was able to teach part time when I received my Master's Degree and was honored to join the staff of Governor's State University as an adjunct professor while I was a state Senator. I taught on Monday evenings a class for the Political Justice Master's Degree program and I loved every minute of it.

Stephanie and Matthew Made it to Adulthood—Easy? You Would Have to Ask Them

Matthew now lives in California and is a Marketing Director for a movie company. Stephanie is the Director of Government Relations and Advocacy for a large hospital system. Her husband, Paul, works in economic development and is a Member of the Champaign City Council. Their daughter, Ellie is now a First grader (2012) at Barkstall Elementary school, loves art classes, reading, cheerleading and gymnastics. My step-daughter Jill Gould and family lives in Chicago, works in the Merchandise Mart and has three children Sydney now in second grade, Sienna who is in preschool and Scott who is seventeen. My step-son Jay is a Major in the Army Special Forces, is married to Ellen and they have a daughter Julia. They live in Florida.

Doing What is Right—Never Easy

As moms, we always want to do the right thing for our children even if it's not clear to us at the time. My kids joined me in Springfield often and they surely learned more than they could have in school alone. My son Matthew got a glimpse of hardball politics during one of his first trips to Springfield. I was summoned into a meeting of gambling lobbyists who wanted to press me to drop my opposition to a gambling bill I had already publicly opposed. This was my first term in office (1997) and Matthew was clearly worried about the way I was being pressured but I stood my ground. I later explained to Matthew that I wasn't going to roll over on a matter of principle no matter how many people were in the room or however long it went. It was all part of his and his sister's education. Standing up for yourself and for what you believe in is something I promised I would do when I arrived in Springfield. That is what I was elected to do. Remember that almost anyone can get elected but not everyone can serve and do the job. Quite a few years later when I was running for reelection to congress (2010) against Adam Kinzinger we were both on a radio station talking about our race and Adam said "being a congressman is easy," not that he would know, he hadn't been elected yet. "All you have to do is vote the right way," he said. I am here to tell you that nothing about being an elected official whatever level it is from School Board to Congress is "easy".

Special University Programs

Along with trying to change the school funding formula to make it more equitable, I worked for years on health care and prescription drug legislation for seniors knowing that success was unlikely until a Democratic governor took office. I had seen my mother suffer from breast cancer without medical insurance for treatment and it made me wonder why all the other industrialized countries of the world managed to provide health care to its citizens, while the US, which spent far more per person for health care was unable to cover millions of its own. Covering basic health needs was an issue I would fight for throughout my political career, from Springfield when I sponsored the *Healthy Illinois* legislation to the battle over Obama's health care legislation.

Senator Jones encouraged me to apply to a three week program at the John F. Kennedy School of Government at Harvard University in 1999. It was called Senior Executives in State and Local Government. Senior executives in state and local governments face greater demands from a skeptical public today than at any time in recent decades.

Across the country, revenues have fallen sharply, the need for services has spiked and trust in government has plummeted. To exercise effective leadership in this difficult environment, officials in government and nonprofit organizations need the knowledge and skills to develop creative solutions under tight constraints and increased public scrutiny. The Senior Executives in State and Local Government program at Harvard University's John F. Kennedy School of Government provides a balance of traditional and hands-on learning experiences to help seasoned public officials meet the changing needs of their constituents and communities. In particular, this program enables participants to become more effective public managers by:

Challenging assumptions about how to exercise leadership in the public sector.
Developing new conceptual frameworks for addressing policy issues.
Examining innovative partnerships and new models of collaborative governance.
Exploring the relationship between citizens and their government.
Understanding the behavioral dimensions of decision-making.
Exchanging ideas with experienced faculty and a diverse group of colleagues.

This three-week program operates as an interactive classroom, where faculty and participants work together on real-life case studies and learn from each other. One of the most frequently cited problems of public officials is how to create and engage in public discourse about difficult subjects. Participants will be in an environment where the classroom serves as a forum for raising difficult issues and practicing the skill of creating and maintaining a conversation that leads to change. Through interactive exercises in the Harvard Decision Science Laboratory, participants will also gain a deeper understanding of their own biases and attitudes as well as personal insights that can sharpen decision making.

It turned out to be enormously helpful to my understanding of the political and legislative process. A true turning point in my political education.

I was also chosen for an Emerging Leaders class at the University of Virginia. The Emerging Leaders Program is designed to enhance the leadership potential and vision of policymakers who are likely to be at the helm of tomorrow's legislatures. Through this unique program, I was able to broaden my perspective and challenge the future in new and positive ways. There were a variety of presentations from leading political leaders combined with cutting-edge leadership concepts from world-renowned faculty. It was programs like these that truly set me on a path to further my political career into what I believe should be a statesman, not a politician.

Interruptions In Life—Never Easy

In 2002, I found myself with a cancer scare. Life had gotten away from me and I missed several years of annual pap smears. When I finally got around to my annual check up, the pap smear came back abnormal. The doctor brushed it off by saying it happens all the time. "Let's just do another test in six months," he said. After the next test the doctor wasn't so optimistic. Everything wasn't ok. My doctor called my cell phone to ask me if I could come to his office because he needed to talk to me. I told him I didn't have time but whatever he had to say he could tell me now. I would just step out of my meeting. He said, "Are you sitting down?" I said, "Yes" (even though I wasn't) and after he uttered the word *cancer* I never heard another word he said. I learned this in September 2002 while I was attending a series of planning meetings at the Olympia Fields Country Club—location of the 2003 US Open (golf) that was coming to my district the following year. I calmly returned to my meeting and sat down. I really wanted to throw up but there was still so much that needed to be done with the US Open right around the corner. I figured I could deal with my doctor and my health later. My immediate concern was resolving the conflict we were having with the Mayor of Olympia Fields, Lindsey Jones and the Cook County Board President, John Stroger, who refused to give us any kind of support financial or otherwise with regards to logistics and security for something that was going to bring so much into our area. I didn't have time to have to figure out what Human Papillomavirus (HPV) was, how did I get HPV, how did it turn into a high risk for cervical cancer, what were the next steps and why did I still feel fine. I had a number of tests to go through, and I also wanted a second opinion, of course. The gynecological oncologist at the University of Chicago gave me several options. He supported my choice for a full hysterectomy especially since there was a family history of cancer. After getting a second opinion, being the non-emotional practical gal that I am, I scheduled the surgery by counting backwards knowing I had to be back in Springfield for veto session in November after the election. I needed six to eight weeks at home to recover, so I booked surgery right then at the University of Chicago without conferring with anyone in my family. I knew they would support me through this challenge and I let a few key friends and staff know what was going on. I even received a few visitors while in the hospital including, a friend who worked there, Michelle Obama.

Standing Up for What You Believe in—Not Easy But ESSENTIAL

A year or so later I was sitting in the audience at a Women in Government conference when during one of the breaks between sessions someone said they were looking for volunteers for a Cervical Cancer Task Force being put together. I jumped at the chance to get involved because as everything started coming back to me I felt the responsibility to share my experience with others. Once I returned home from the conference armed with all this new information on how we could eradicate cervical cancer, legislators of both parties wanted nothing to do with me on this issue, calling it too controversial. I just wanted to educate the public about cervical cancer and the human papillomavirus (HPV). I thought of myself as somewhat intelligent and I had been completely blindsided when my doctor told me that because by body was unable to get rid of the HP virus that I was now at a very high risk for cervical cancer. I didn't want anyone else to go through that. According to www.womenshealth.gov the purpose of the pap smear is to check for cervical cancer and it is the human papillomavirus that causes cervical cancer. If it meant I had to be a punching bag for a while, so be it. In the end, I was able to pass SB 937 which became Public Act 095-0422. This bill requires insurance companies to cover the HPV vaccine and if the girl is under the age of eighteen and the family has no insurance, the Department of Public Health must cover the cost of the vaccine because of the *All Kids* insurance program. It also requires doctor's offices to have pamphlets available on HPV to give to families for educational purposes. I was adamant this was not going to turn into something that only the rich or those with insurance had access to. If we were going to eradicate cervical cancer, anyone who wanted the HPV vaccine or further testing was going to be able to have it and since I knew there was a possibility we could eliminate a cancer someday I never wanted a granddaughter of mine who knew I was in a position to change the law to ask me someday why I didn't do something I had the power to change.

Barack Had His Detractors

In his first few years in the state Senate, Obama gradually won over many of his colleagues who at first saw him as an upstart outsider from Harvard University. An exception was Senator Rickey Hendon, a loud outspoken African American politico from Chicago's West Side who seemed to enjoy baiting Obama in skirmishes that took on a personal tone. Obama was known for his cool, calm and collectedness but he sure came close to tossing that out the window one evening in late May when tensions were high and Hendon had no problem getting on a person's last nerve anyway. There was a bill that closed down several Department of Children and Family Services facilities in the Chicagoland area to consolidate services and one of them was in Rickey's district. Having not heard anything for or against the bill, Barack voted yes like most of the other senators. The bill passed and all of a sudden Rickey Hendon asks for permission to speak publicly. Once he had command of the microphone he let Barack "have it" like only Rickey could. They didn't call him "Hollywood Hendon" for nothing. There were several minutes of back and forth between the two of them with Barack basically telling Senator Hendon that he never heard from Rickey. All he would have had to do was tell Barack he wanted him to vote no and he would have done that for the Senator but Rickey just wouldn't let it go, this time hitting a bit below the belt by saying Barack should have known that the "brothers" were sticking together opposing the bill. Barack left his seat and walked over to speak to Rickey. I really thought for a moment they were going to "take it outside" but luckily Barack thought better of letting Rickey drag him down to his level and cooler heads prevailed. I was surprised Leader Jones never stepped in, instead seemed to almost enjoy the back and forth, like watching who would prevail in a prizefight from his seat on the floor.

Jones knew his leadership team well and later, as Senate President, he found ways to use our different talents and temperaments to serve his legislative agenda. He would ask me to be in the chair to preside when he wanted a full discussion of issues and needed someone who was willing to give Republicans a chance to speak. If he felt that time was of the essence and Republicans were being unnecessarily obstructive, he would send Rickey Hendon to preside. "He's meaner than you are Debbie," he would explain.

Obama's First Political Defeat

In 2000, Barack Obama experienced his first political defeat, when he ran for Congress against Cong Bobby Rush a defeat many now admit was a blessing in disguise. Barack acknowledged this was one of those races in which everything that could go wrong did. As Obama was making mistakes they were compounded by tragedy. Rush's adult son was shot to death by drug dealers causing a wave of sympathy and then Senator Obama missed a high profile vote on the *Safe*

Neighborhoods Act when his daughter got sick while on a family trip to Hawaii. Bobby Rush made sure everyone knew he wasn't impressed with Barack's Harvard education. Obama's detractors said he was "too white and too bright" because of his association with the two strongholds of white power: Harvard and University of Chicago. Obama hadn't quite figured out retail politics and his professorial style did not always serve him well in a tough race against the incumbent Congressman Bobby Rush, the former Black Panther, who represented the impoverished Englewood area on the south and southwest side of Chicago. The most important reasons for Obama's defeat, however, was that there were few differences between the two men on the issues, and Bobby Rush was better known at the time, even though he had just run for Mayor of Chicago and was crushed my Mayor Rich Daley. Obama and Senator Donne Trotter who also ran in the primary felt Rush would be vulnerable, but wasn't. Rush also picked up the endorsement of President Bill Clinton who was popular in the African American community. Clinton did commercials for the incumbent and even though Obama complained profusely about it people understood that Rush had backed Clinton during impeachment proceedings and Clinton was simply returning the favor.

Losing in a three way primary race for congress wasn't taken lightly by someone as ambitious as Barack Obama and it really set him back for quite a while. His defeat also forced him to rethink his approach to campaigning and helped him realize he needed to develop a more personal campaign style that was not easy for him to do. It didn't happen overnight, but by the time he ran for US Senate four years later, Obama had vastly improved his ability to communicate with the voters.

Two years after Obama's defeat, we were looking forward to having a Democratic governor to work with to pass urgent legislation that never had a chance while we were in the minority under governors Jim Edgar and George Ryan. The newly elected governor was Rod Blagojevich who had been a congressman representing the Northwest side of Chicago. Unfortunately, much of what followed would remind me of the saying "be careful what you wish for."

Making History

As Obama was becoming our US Senator in 2004, I was becoming the first female in Illinois to serve as Majority Leader making my own history. As I reflect back to 1997 when as freshmen state Senators we both seemed to know what we wanted. I always had my eye on leadership within my caucus and Barack was focused like a laser on national politics and so far we had both been moving along as planned.

The excitement was electric on February 10, 2007 when most of us braved the below zero cold watching Obama decide to get into the Presidential race. After US Senator Dick Durbin introduced Barack, my colleagues in the Senate and I who were all keeping each other warm for hours instantly started thawing out when Barack started talking to each one of us in the crowd with these words.

> Let me begin by saying thanks to all you who've traveled, from far and wide, to brave the cold today.
>
> We all made this journey for a reason. It's humbling, but in my heart I know you didn't come here just for me, you came here because you believe in what this country can be. In the face of war, you believe there can be peace. In the face of despair, you believe there can be hope. In the face of a politics that's shut you out, that's told you to settle, that's divided us for too long, you believe we can be one people, reaching for what's possible, building that more perfect union.
>
> That's the journey we're on today. But let me tell you how I came to be here. As most of you know, I am not a native of this great state. I moved to Illinois over two decades ago. I was a young man then, just a year out of college; I knew no one in Chicago, was without money or family connections. But a group of churches had offered me a job as a community organizer for $13,000 a year. And I accepted the job, sight unseen, motivated then by a single, simple, powerful idea—that I might play a small part in building a better America.

4

You Gotta Pay to Play

If you don't change what you are doing today, all of your tomorrows will look like yesterday
—Jim Rohn

Following his nationally publicized arrest at home and subsequent conviction for bribery schemes, Rod Blagojevich would become a flamboyant symbol of Illinois' corruption. It is easy to forget that his administration's disregard for the law and the practice of pay-to-play differed little from the two previous governors, Jim Edgar and George Ryan. *Chicago Tribune* columnist, John Kass, calls the top leadership of Illinois "The Combine" to describe the bipartisan cooperation which has enriched political insiders no matter which party was in power. My experiences as a member of the state Senate only strengthened my belief that ethics legislation and campaign finance reform were some of the most important issues we confronted. As Cindy Canary of the Illinois Committee for Political Reform put it in an interview with *Illinois Issues Magazine,* "Why do we need campaign finance reform? Because this is the issue behind every issue that we care about." I became close with Cindy as well as Jim Kales of the Illinois Committee for Political Reform. Jim and a camera crew were at my campaign headquarters on election night in 1996 after I defeated Aldo DeAngelis to celebrate our win since my opponent was the poster child for everything that was wrong with money in politics. The other group that was very involved in campaign finance reform was Protestants for the Common Good and I became close with John Mcllwain. Cindy, Jim, John and I saw a lot of one another since we were bound and determined to do something about reform. I couldn't believe the resistance from those in office to fixing a system that obvious was causing the electorate to lose confidence in not only the system, but also with the politicians themselves.

In some ways, I found Jim Edgar—the only one of the three governors I served with who was not convicted of a crime—to be the least likable. Edgar had won the election in 1994 by handily defeating Dawn Clark Netsch, a highly respected former state senator and state comptroller, who was deeply involved in reform politics. For this very reason, Netsch got little support from the regular Democratic organization in Chicago, which was an insurmountable disadvantage in a statewide race. "Not just another pretty face" was her slogan, which sought to portray Edgar's good looks as his only advantage over a woman whose wisdom and experience ultimately proved less important to the voters. I had campaigned for Netsch when she visited the South Suburbs and I introduced her around. She had graduated first in her law class at Northwestern University and was a popular professor and well regarded attorney. She prevailed in the Democratic primary with a simple campaign commercial "Straight Shooter" showcasing her talents as a pool player to highlight her message. Both Netsch and Edgar had promised to reform education funding by lessening the dependence on property taxes and replacing part of the property taxes with an income tax, but, at the last minute Edgar switched his position to accommodate his wealthy constituents who were upset that they might have to pay more money if the education system moved to the income tax.

Governor Edgar

Governor Edgar managed to become popular by simply saying "no" to legislation that might create waves or discomfort for his supporters. Edgar held on to his political capital by leaving in place a system that rewarded powerful and corrupt political insiders like William Cellini, the shadowy Springfield fixer extraordinaire for both political parties who managed to avoid indictments while becoming a multi-millionaire on questionable deals that gouged the taxpayers. Finally, jurors convicted Cellini in 2011 of conspiring to squeeze a Hollywood producer for a $1.5 million donation to Blagojevich's campaign. Cellini thought he could use his influence to yank millions of pension dollars from an investment company this producer owned. US District Judge, James Zagel, decided to delay Cellini's sentencing scheduled for October 4, 2012, because the seventy-seven year old reportedly suffered a heart attack and was too ill to travel to Chicago. Under Edgar, Cellini's sweet, typically generous Italian sister, Janice, served as Governor Edgar's patronage chief. Edgar managed to avoid federal indictments but was forced to testify in bribery trials which convicted a major campaign contributor, Michael Martin, and a former state welfare administrator, Ronald Lowder, who contributed more than $250,000 to Governor Edgar's campaigns. Martin's firm won a major contract with the Department of Public Aid after showering state officials with gifts including trips to Germany, Mexico and the Superbowl.

Whatever Edgar's general popularity he was a remote, aloof figure to the legislators in both parties except for a few insiders. This became even clearer to me when I attended the funeral for Republican Illinois Senator Harry "Babe" Woodyard who died on January 31,1997 of a massive stroke. Governor Edgar sat at a restaurant table at the lunch speaking only with his body guards, not even acknowledging Republican legislators grieving for their colleague who were sitting nearby. Within earshot, I could hear Republican senators complain bitterly about his aloofness.

I suspected that an ethics reform bill with teeth was unlikely to pass under Jim Edgar, but I drafted them anyway with input from Cindy Canary from the Illinois Campaign for Political Reform, John Mcllwain from the Protestants for a Common Good and one of my mentors, respected former legislator Tony Scariano who had become a judge. Judge Scariano had taken me under his wing when I became a senator in 1997. We would go to lunch about once a month at Three Star, an Italian restaurant in "da heights"(Chicago Heights, Illinois) so he could educate me on the workings of the legislature. Those "workings" were usually in the form of stories that I will forever treasure. I am thankful to Justice Scariano for sharing them with me.

Senate President James "Pate" Philip, (R) made it clear that serious ethics bills would never get out of committee. Nor would I have any luck with my prescription drug bill for senior citizens which was a passion of mine. Pate was old school and the boss of highly Republican DuPage County west of Chicago, which was the mirror image of the Cook County Democratic machine, a place where election chicanery reigned and insiders were rewarded with patronage and contracts. The late Chicago columnist, Mike Royko, once described Pate as "a suburban polyester jerk" but I doubt the former Marine cared much what anyone thought of him. I made repeated requests to Leader Phillip's chief of staff, Carter Hendren, about scheduling a meeting with the Senate President to discuss my prescription drug or ethics bills and Hendren would answer snidely, "What year?" Philip and Hendren were Edgar's top operatives and they personified his approach to most members of the legislature.

Fortunately, former US Senator Paul Simon, who founded the Illinois Public Policy Institute at Southern Illinois University in Carbondale, Illinois, after his US Senate term expired had both the stature and a connection to the Republican governor that helped those of us in the legislature chip away at Illinois' well-deserved reputation as the "Wild West" of campaign financing. By the mid-1990's, this issue was getting increased public attention. The Springfield State *Journal-Register* did a ground breaking investigation comparing data bases of campaign contributions and state contracts which found that between 1991 and 1992, during Governor Edgar's first term, at least fourteen thousand contracts combined were worth $1.6 billion had been awarded to individuals or businesses who contributed to statewide candidates in the 1990 election.

To soften the Edgar administration's refusal to consider campaign finance reform, Paul Simon shrewdly hired Mike Lawrence, a respected former statehouse reporter, who was then an advisor and press secretary for Governor Edgar. When

George Ryan was governor, Senate President Pate Philip finally gave in and Mike Lawrence was able to persuade both Hendren and Philip to appoint a couple of Republican leaders to join a bipartisan working group to find areas of agreement on campaign finance reform.

Republican Senator Kirk Dillard and then freshman Senator Barack Obama, were the two senators who helped put together the *State Gift Ban Act* of 1998 to limit pay-to-play abuses. On one hand, the bill's electronic campaign reporting requirements were a widely hailed important step in creating transparency and easy access to records. On the other hand, the *State Gift Ban Act* was very porous and contained some five pages of exceptions. A good deal more work is needed to be done to tackle pay-to-play in Illinois. The next strong impetus for that would come after Jim Edgar's successor Governor George Ryan was indicted on corruption charges.

Governor Ryan

George Ryan, who was elected governor in 1998, was as likable and accessible as his predecessor, Jim Edgar, had been cold and distant. The pharmacist from Kankakee had turned two family owned drugstores into a chain of pharmacies, Ryan was down to earth, friendly and unpretentious. There was never a problem getting a meeting with him to discuss state business. Like Edgar, Ryan had served as a legislator and secretary of state before becoming governor. Ryan, however, had also held the position of lieutenant governor. George Ryan's word could also be counted on in contrast to his successor, Rod Blagojevich. We didn't need a memorandum of understanding when we reached an agreement with him; a handshake was good enough. Governor Ryan also opened up the governor's mansion on occasions to legislative leaders so we could gather together informally to talk about developments and socialize. His wife, Lura Lynn, whom he met in high school, would greet guests at the door. Governor Ryan also liked having small groups of friends over for dinner. One evening Governor Ryan had about six of us legislators over for an Italian dinner. Other than myself, dinner guests were Senators Dillard, Molaro and Deleo. Representative Skip Saviano was known throughout Springfield for his delicious Italian cooking, so of course he was designated as chef. The governor enjoyed his time with us. The Italians (I didn't even have to remind the governor my maiden name was DeFrancesco) taught everyone else at the table what real food was. By ten o'clock we had eaten all the food, smoked all the cigars and drank all we could.

It was time to leave but as we all started getting up from the table, the governor had the hook out and said "Hold on a minute, I think we can probably find another bottle of Grand Marnier," insisting the group stick around for just one more nightcap which we did.

Unlike his predecessor, Ryan committed substantial state funding for transportation, education and technology infrastructure. He was the one who suggested fee and tax increases to fund the large transportation, infrastructure bill. He was able to get many of his Republican colleagues to go along with it A Democrat governor probably would never have gotten the support of Republicans therefore something like that would have been dead on arrival. When one of the legislators who opposed the tax increases used to fund the infrastructure improvements took credit for the projects, Ryan did not hesitate to call him out. Ryan also demonstrated a surprising disregard for public opinion, like meeting with Fidel Castro to discuss humanitarian aid, despite protests by anti-Castro groups.

The issue that brought Ryan national attention however, was his decision to declare a moratorium on the death penalty for individuals who had been sentenced to die. There is every reason to believe that Ryan made the decision on the basis of substantial evidence that several death row inmates were the victims of wrongful convictions. With only two days before a scheduled execution, attorneys for an inmate named Anthony Porter, who had spent fifteen years on death row won a stay because he was mentally disabled. Porter then was exonerated as the result of work of the Innocence Project at Northwestern University which uncovered evidence showing he was innocent. Another man, Alstory Simon, admitted his guilt and pleaded guilty for the crime that Porter had been convicted. Under Ryan, a total of thirteen wrongfully convicted inmates were released after appealing their cases based on new evidence. Increasingly, it became clear to Ryan that while convictions are reversible when new evidence comes to light, death is always irreversible.

This was not an abstract concern to Ryan, but a call for action that required a moratorium on executions. Upon leaving office, he went further by commuting the sentences of one hundred and sixty-seven inmates from death row to life in prison because of his belief that surely innocent people were being put to death. In addition, the governor pardoned four of the death row inmates who were convicted as a result of police torture. While Ryan's actions were applauded by anti-death penalty groups nationally and internationally, it is safe to say that most of his Republican brethren and many Democrats opposed these actions. I agreed with the governor's decision on the moratorium.

Unfortunately, George Ryan was also a prisoner of the corrupt way business was all too often conducted in Illinois. Near the end of the governor's first term a lengthy investigation of corruption during his term as secretary of state was generating scores of federal indictments and kept reaching higher into the governor's own office. A strong impetus for these investigations was the shocking story behind the deaths of the six Willis children in a horrible car accident in Wisconsin, the fault of a truck driver who obtained his license illegally through a bribe scheme at the Illinois Secretary of State's office.

The governor decided not to run again, which was probably a wise decision. Before leaving office, however, he sent the legislature a budget which included plum assignments for members of his staff. It was the old way of doing business, practiced by Republicans and Democrats alike, but I had no problem voting against these perks at a time when the state could not afford them. This would not be fair to the taxpayers!

In March of 2003, just two months after leaving office, Ryan was hit by a twenty-two count federal indictment alleging that he and family members were rewarded with vacations and cash for steering millions in contracts to friends and for blocking an investigation into the bribes for licenses scheme. Because I liked George Ryan personally, appreciated his accessibility and some of his accomplishments, I've been repeatedly asked how I felt about his conviction and six-year sentence. Certainly I felt bad for Ryan and especially his wife, Lura Lynn, a sweet lady who died of cancer in June of 2011. I was Governor Ryan's state Senator however and as wonderful as their family is, it is especially important that elected officials are held to the highest of standards. If that means they spend time in federal prison that is the price that must be paid for corrupting the political process that robs citizens of honest government.

Governor Blagojevich

When Rod Blagojevich was inaugurated in 2003, Republican governors had controlled the governor's mansion in Illinois for almost thirty years and Democratic legislators were very excited about a new era in government and the chance to pass legislation that had always been blocked by Republicans. In the Democrat primary for governor, I had supported Blagojevich's opponent, Paul Vallas, who had earned a good reputation for upgrading the Chicago school system. I also didn't think the Blagojevich name would carry well in downstate Illinois. However, it turned out Blagojevich proved infinitely more charismatic than Vallas. His populist message, combined with his pledge not to raise taxes, helped Blagojevich become a winner in both the primary and the general election in 2002. Even though I had supported his opponent in the primary, Blagojevich greeted me warmly on election night and like almost all the Democrat legislators, I looked forward to working with the new administration.

Rod Blagojevich carried the seeds of his eventual downfall into the governor's office, but it is also true that it was hard to get cooperation between all the Democrats that controlled most of Springfield. This lack of cooperation made getting anything done more difficult and damaged the functioning and fiscal health of the state of Illinois. In the early days of his administration, Blagojevich sought regular meetings with legislative leaders including both Emil Jones who was about to become Senate President, and Speaker Madigan who was the only one who would not attend these meetings.

Speaker Madigan

"While other legislative leaders play checkers, Mike Madigan plays three dimensional chess" wrote veteran statehouse journalist, Charlie Wheeler, in *Illinois*

Issues. No one in Springfield doubted Madigan's discipline and political acumen, but it was repeatedly used to protect and promote his own power. Important state issues would come and go and Madigan could switch his positions with ease, as long as they strengthened his power base. I was told by a reliable source that House Democrat members with independent thoughts or legislative goals different than those of the Speaker could find themselves without funds or staff. People complained for years that pressing state issues could wait or remain unsolved for years, if it impinged in any way on Madigan not getting it done his way. Madigan helped his daughter, Lisa, become Illinois Attorney General in 2003 with an outpouring of contributions from the speaker's own donor base, i.e., companies and individuals who understood that a contribution to the speaker's daughter was like an insurance policy for their legislative goals. While Lisa Madigan made more than a name for herself on consumer issues, she refrained from investigations of political corruption despite an over abundance of low hanging fruit which was left for US Attorney, Patrick Fitzgerald, to harvest. The only major exception to Attorney General Madigan's lack of interest in political corruption was when she began to investigate Blagojevich, her father's nemesis, only to receive a firm request from the US Attorney to withdraw and allow his federal investigation to proceed. Lisa Madigan is a very popular attorney general and would most likely win whatever position she sought to run for if she chose to leave that office. She was encouraged to run for the US Senate seat vacated by Barack Obama but chose not to. She could have run for governor in the Democrat primary, but the general consensus is that Illinois is not big enough for two Madigans at the top. Mike Madigan would probably have to retire first and there is no indication that is going to happen any time soon.

Chicago Politics

Political control in the state of Illinois has its tribal aspects and the South Side Irish have been the most powerful of the tribes with Richard J. Daley and his son, Richard M. Daley, dominating the mayor's office over a sixty-year period. It is yet to be seen where the new Chicago Mayor, Rahm Emanuel, falls into the picture coming from the north side of the city. During his campaign it was well known that he and Alderman Burke went round and round because of the Alderman's possesive support for Gery Chico during the mayoral election. Supposedly it was Burke who put down the groundwork for the residency challenge that nearly knocked the former White House chief of staff off the ballot. Emanuel then stated before the election if elected he was thinking of reorganizing the city council with regards to possibly eliminating Burke's body guards and Finance Committee chairmanship. None of that ever happened and supposedly they have put their differences aside. Ed Burke, the most powerful city councilman and the powerful Speaker of the House Mike Madigan, who is also the Chairman of the Illinois Democrat party dominate the selection of judges. Blagojevich, a two term congressman and state legislator, did not fit into this group on any level. Neither did north side Alderman Richard Mell, who became the driving force of Rod Blagojevich's campaign for governor rounding up regular Democrats across the state with little help from Madigan. He did get help from powerful north side committeemen and legislator Jimmy Deleo whose allegiance was to Alderman Mell, not Blagojevich.

Those who had observed and dealt with Speaker Madigan over the years understood that he was likely to do as little as possible to help the new governor succeed despite his role as Illinois Democrat party chairman. Veteran *Sun-Times* political columnist, Lynn Sweet, wrote later that Madigan, "shows little interest in doing the job of state party chairman" and has "used the position mainly to reelect his state House members and to help daughter, Lisa Madigan . . . Unlike every other state party chairman in the nation, Madigan refuses to run a viable statewide political organization."

Speaker Madigan had become quite comfortable as the only top Democrat leader in the general assembly while Republicans controlled the governor's office and Illinois state Senate. Being the top Democrat in Springfield gave Madigan considerable power. Governor Ryan and Pate Philip had to come to him for support. The 2002 election of Blagojevich as governor and Emil Jones as Illinois Senate President changed this dynamic. It meant that Madigan was no longer the only high level Democrat leader–a situation he did not like being in. With a healthy Democrat majority in his chamber, Madigan still had the power to block legislation and halt the legislative process if he chose to do so in order to prevail. The new Democrat governor and the Illinois Senate President would have to meet Madigan on his own terms, or government would grind to a halt and it increasingly did.

5

Obama Almost Didn't Make It To Boston

Courage is grace under pressure
—Ernest Hemingway

Illinois State Budget—2004

May thirty-first of each year is the date all legislation and a budget must pass in Illinois. Anything after that needs a three-fifths majority to pass. The Senate had the necessary three fifths but the House didn't have the seventy votes needed in their chamber to avoid bringing the House Republicans into the negotiations. So in 2004 you would think Speaker Madigan, Senate President Jones and Governor Blagojevich would have wanted to get the budget *agreed* upon and leave town shortly after midnight, the thirty-first of May. The budget we did pass received the support of the House and the Senate. We lacked the third branch of government: the Executive Branch. The Governor wanted $300 million more for education and the legislature said their wasn't any more money in the budget to give it to him. Blagojevich just couldn't get it in his head that in Illinois the budget had to balance. He had come from the US House of Representatives where that wasn't the case. So Blagojevich started calling daily special sessions. By keeping the entire legislature stuck in Springfield Blagojevich thought the legislators would get so angry they would put pressure on their leaders to sit down together and work out their budget differences. Pressure or no pressure, that did not happen. What did happen was a very hot summer in Springfield where one special session day ran into the next well into July. Governor Blagojevich and Speaker Madigan, who is also the chairman of the Democrat party in Illinois, almost prevented Barack

Obama from getting to the Democratic convention in Boston to give the speech of his life that put him on a path that made him a national figure which ultimately set him on the road to the White House. Obama's friends in the Senate all knew he was writing, rewriting and practicing his speech while we waited for some agreement on a budget deal that would allow those of us who were delegates to get on a plane to Boston.

Barack Had Luck and a Lot of It

A combination of luck, disciplined fundraising and some legislative successes had propelled Obama to the Democratic nomination for US Senate. Better known candidates had decided not to run including the incumbent Republican Senator Peter Fitzgerald and his Democratic predecessor Carol Mosely Braun. Obama's luck then continued when the candidacy of his strongest opponent in the general election, Republican Jack Ryan, imploded after his estranged wife Jeri, a former actress, accused him of pressuring her to have sex in front of strangers at swingers clubs in New York, New Orleans and Paris. Republicans had to import a candidate, African American conservative gadfly, Alan Keyes from Maryland to run against Obama in the 2004 general election. Talk about luck! I am sure Barack was tired of people asking him to buy lottery tickets for them because of all the ongoing luck he was having.

Barack's Strong Credentials

Meanwhile, Obama had burnished his political credentials by taking a strong stand in opposition to the war in Iraq. Emil Jones had arranged for Obama to chair the Senate Health and Human Services Committee and Obama had gotten credit for bills that regulated racial profiling and made Illinois the first state to videotape homicide interrogations. Obama had worked closely with the police organizations to pass a comprehensive bill on death penalty reforms. Almost miraculously, Obama had managed to persuade Democratic Presidential candidate Senator John Kerry to let him give the keynote address at the National Democratic Convention. The table was set for a historic moment but now all of that appeared in jeopardy; because the delegates, the legislature and the people of Illinois, were being held hostage to a political feud between Governor Blagojevich and Speaker Madigan. Not only did the governor and the speaker not get along there was wide speculation that this may even have something to do with all the attention Senate President Emil Jones, Jr. was getting for Obama's success.

Because Obama was running for the US Senate he could not afford to be absent when these crucial votes were taking place. Barack had missed votes during a special session that was called a few years earlier by then Governor Ryan regarding major gun legislation referred to as the *Safe Neighborhoods Act*. His absence was because of his decision not to return from his Christmas vacation trip to Hawaii, and he couldn't go through that again.

Senate colleagues would see him pacing the floor, most likely practicing his speech in his head. He pleaded with Senate President Emil Jones to find a way to end the gridlock in time for the convention but Jones couldn't because the feud was between the Governor and the Speaker. Seeing his concern, state Senator John Cullerton kidded Barack by saying "Hey you've got to spend more time on that speech I wrote for you anyway. You want to become a star don't you?"

I Was Brought in to Facilitate

Madigan, who would be leading the delegation to the convention and was holding things up, said publicly that he wasn't concerned about when any of the delegates arrived in Boston, or if we made it at all. No one knew if he was bluffing or not because it was a known fact Madigan didn't enjoy these kind of things. As Assistant Senate Majority leader at the time, I was usually the one presiding over the special sessions, conducting the business of the Senate going from negotiating sessions to special hearings and caucuses. It was basically perfunctory because nothing of substance was going on except the usual rants from the Republicans as to how long this charade would continue. As usual, the amount to be spent on education funding and how it would be distributed were the issues of controversy with the wealthy school districts wanting to maintain the status quo and the under-funded districts looking for a fairer shake and better opportunity for their students. The leaders were still $300 million apart with change nowhere on the horizon. At one point, the governor's staff called me in to moderate what they feared would be a very contentious budget hearing, sending me a hard hat with the words "Senator-the-Hammer-Debbie" printed on it.

Around this time, I wrote in my journal asking rhetorically why the people of Illinois should suffer because the Speaker did not want to meet with the Governor and negotiate a budget but the same thing could be said about the Governor not signing the budget the House and the Senate had agreed on before the legislative deadline. The Governor called a special session every day which meant no one was supposed to return home. Eventually sessions were set up so legislators could leave on Saturday late morning and return late Sunday. Governor Blagojevich didn't have to spend days and weeks on end in Springfield because he had access to a state plane to fly him back and forth each day which was estimated to cost the taxpayers $5,800 each round trip. I have to wonder how many special session days he would have called if he had to stay in Springfield like the rest of us. Every day Barack would ask me if we thought today would be the day (when there would be a deal). No such luck as I brought each special session in and then out again without any good news regarding a deal. Blagojevich and Madigan's disgust for one another had created an unnecessary delay that made the Democratic party, which he served as nominal leader, look very disorganized. We were still stuck in Springfield waiting around for "those in charge" to put all the pieces in place as the clock began to run down for our timely flight to the Democratic convention. Problem was the "top four" plus the governor were not even meeting and many of the members were so angry they went home telling the governor, "Go ahead send the state police after me." The delays set a record for the longest session in thirty years.

Finally: A Deal

It wasn't until the twenty-fifth of July that a deal was finally made; just in time to get on a plane the next morning to get to Boston. Believe it or not there never was any change in the $300 million difference in education funding. I was able to drive home in the pounding rain arriving home at eleven o'clock that evening and getting up at four o'clock in the morning to make the morning flight from Chicago's Midway airport to Boston along with Senator Durbin and his wife, Loretta and many of Illinois' top Democrats. There was a collective sigh of relief that we were all on the plane on our way to Boston.

The Speech

Before Barack Obama gave his keynote speech at the convention, there were many convention delegates in Boston who had no idea who he was. I was wearing an Obama for US Senate button and I was asked if I was from *Alabama*. I responded that the button said "Obama, not Alabama." After thanking Senator Durbin for his introduction, Obama invited a national audience to see his own story as proof of America's greatness:

> "Tonight is a particular honor for me because—let's face it—my presence on this stage is pretty unlikely. My father was a foreign student, born and raised in a small village in Kenya. He grew up herding goats, went to school in a tin-roof shack. His father—my grandfather—was a cook, a domestic servant to the British . . . But my grandfather had larger dreams for his son. Through hard work and perseverance my father got a scholarship to study in a magical place, America, that shone as a beacon of freedom and opportunity to so many who had come before.
>
> While studying here, my father met my mother. She was born in a town on the other side of the world, in Kansas. Her father worked on oil rigs and farms through most of the Depression. The day after Pearl Harbor my grandfather signed up for duty; joined Patton's army, marched across Europe. Back home, my grandmother raised their baby and went to work on a bomber assembly line. After the war, they studied on the G.I. Bill, bought a house through FHA, and later moved west all the way to Hawaii in search of opportunity . . . I stand here today, grateful for the diversity of my heritage, aware that my parents' dreams live on in my two precious daughters. I stand here knowing that my story is part of the larger American story, that I owe a debt to all of those who came before me, and that, in no other country on earth, is my story even possible . . ."

Most people, however, would remember the call to resist divisions that set Americans of different political stripes against each other:

> "Now even as we speak, there are those who are preparing to divide us, the spin masters, the negative ad peddlers who embrace the politics of anything goes. Well, I say to them tonight, there is not a liberal America and a conservative America—there is the United States of America. There is not a Black America and a White America and Latino America and Asian America—there's the United States of America."

The response to the speech was thunderous. I noticed Terry Link, our colleague who was also elected in 1996 had tears in his eyes. None of us said anything, we just stared straight ahead not sure what we just heard and from whom. I was watching the crowd go crazy for a guy they didn't even know, but from listening to his speech felt like they could relate to him. They all felt the electricity; they didn't need to know him. The convention delegates who had asked us about Barack Obama earlier, were now constantly beseeching us for the Obama buttons we were wearing. We couldn't keep the buttons on, the demand was so strong from people who felt that Barack Obama was on his way to bigger things. Some people have questioned whether Obama was either naive about overcoming divisions or disingenuous in his condemnation of bitterly divisive politics.

The Difference Between Republicans

Unfortunately, the positive experiences Barack had in the Illinois state Senate may have proved misleading when he began his presidency expecting to find common ground with congressional Republicans. As a result, he may have waited too long to conclude that he was facing Republican leaders like Senate Minority Leader Mitch McConnell and House Speaker John Boehner whose overriding goal was to see him fail-whatever affect that might have on a country that was reeling from a deep recession.

Members from both parties used to play golf together, and on occasion the families socialized. The House was run on a partisan basis, but it wasn't the cutthroat politics of today. There was civility but it has gone. Some of the actions are not only petty, they are completely counterproductive.

I was there while the Democrats controlled the House. Those who were there when the Republicans controlled Congress said that the Democrats controlled things differently. Not because they were more civic minded, but because of their nature. The Democrat party was much more diverse and it was harder for leadership to impose discipline like the Republicans could.

Like Obama, my experience working with Republicans in Illinois was mostly positive, which is what I later found so frustrating about the hyper-partisanship I came across in Washington.

6

Downfall of Another Governor

Do not follow where the path may lead . . . Go instead where there is no path and leave a trail.
—Ralph Waldo Emerson

"You know, I should have f–n' looked the other way on the landfill and then my father-in-law would take care of us. I should have f–n' done that."
—Former Governor Rod Blagojevich on a FBI tape.

When Rod Blagojevich first took office as Illinois Governor, it was not immediately clear where he stood on ethics legislation. He talked reform, which was what a public weary of the Ryan administration's scandals and indictments wanted to hear. Still, it was well known that while Blagojevich's charisma had taken him across the finish line, it was his father-in-law Richard Mell's old guard patronage army that had done the heavy lifting, not just in Chicago, but across the state.

Alderman Dick Mell (Blagojevich's Father-in-Law)

To say that Alderman Mell was a quintessential Chicago ward boss barely does justice to the 33rd Ward; as an alderman he provided superior service to his constituents, while using hardball tactics and intimidation against any political adversaries. On the one hand, Mell took on the landlords that abused the rights of his tenants, set up Graffiti Busters, a program that was a model for other wards, and arranged special garbage pick ups for constituents who were disposing of old furniture. The alderman could sometimes be found following the garbage truck and tossing furniture pieces into the truck. Hard pressed residents of the ward could call on the alderman for help with a problem and count on Mell's assistance. On the other hand, Mell's political forces had a reputation for thug-like tactics against opposition candidates and their supporters. This was typified by Mell's precinct captain Dominic Longo who was convicted of vote fraud in the 1984 gubernatorial election and suspected of extortion and ghost payrolls. Longo had once been accused of pulling a gun and threatening to shoot an elderly resident of the ward if he didn't take down a sign of Mell's opponent. No charges were ever brought against Longo and the incident was shrugged off by Mell who said, "Dominic gets blamed for a lot of things, but he wouldn't be that stupid."

Mell's crucial help in making Blagojevich a congressman and then the first Democrat governor in twenty-six years enhanced Mell's reputation as a kingmaker. That was perhaps more important to Mell than any favor the governor might eventually do for his father-in-law. Meanwhile, Mell's lieutenant, Dominic Longo, formed an organization called the Citizens for Better Government, which ran an advertisement on Blagojevich's behalf during the gubernatorial campaign. Blagojevich had publicly praised Longo despite his dubious record. Once Blagojevich was elected governor, however, Mell and his associates say Blagojevich began immediately distancing his administration from his father-in-law and the 33rd Ward Organization. There was speculation that Blagojevich was cutting his ties to Mell and embracing reform because he hoped to be taken seriously as a future presidential candidate. He hired a Washington, DC consulting firm to guide him. The perceived lack of gratitude from his son-in-law was sure to anger a proud individual like Richard Mell. It was one thing to distance himself from his father-in-law's patronage armies; it was another to go out of his way to make life more difficult for his mentor and most powerful patron, but that was the path the new governor took.

At the time, I had no idea that two bills I sponsored would play a role in bringing down Governor Blagojevich. The first was strictly aimed at regulating landfills and their owners (the other being the ethics bill). For several years I had been negotiating with the Illinois Environmental Protection Agency (IEPA) to tighten restrictions on a very large landfill in my district that we suspected was illegally dumping without a proper license. I was pleased but somewhat surprised to learn that the governor was interested in joining me on my bill. Maybe Blagojevich was going to take the reform side after all since this bill had serious restrictions barring landfill ownership by relatives of top state officials and it gave the Illinois EPA power to shut down landfills that were deemed a threat to public health or the environment. The legislation applied to all landfills across the state of Illinois and it would have been very difficult to pass without widespread support.

Public Spats Can Be Very Nasty

At the time, there was no way of my knowing the governor's father-in-law and a distant relative, Frank Schmidt, owned a landfill in Joliet, Illinois, or that Blagojevich was targeting them specifically in my bill. Nor did I know the landfill would be the final straw in the relationship between the governor and his politically powerful father in-law. Once my bill became law a feud broke out in full force because Blagojevich and his administration accused Schmidt of accepting illegal waste and of "using his ties to the Blagojevich family to solicit" business for an illegal-dumping operation. The governor ordered the dump shut down.

Humiliated, Alderman Mell responded angrily to the governor's involvement in my bill and claimed Blagojevich was going out of his way to target him [Mell] on the mistaken notion that he had a financial interest in the Joliet landfill. Alderman Mell didn't stop there claiming that the governor's top fundraiser, Chris Kelly, was selling jobs for campaign contributions of $50,000 each. Showing the full extent of his anger in dramatic fashion, Alderman Mell portrayed himself to the *Chicago Sun-Times* as the loyal wife who'd been dumped for a trophy wife by the governor:

> *"Now he's at the top, and he says, 'What a great man I am,' and she says, 'Wait a second, I remember when you were crying that we needed more money, or you were crying because you thought you'd fail one of the tests.' He, with his gigantic ego cannot stand that anymore. So he jettisons that wife, and he gets a new trophy wife. I am the old wife. The new wife is Chris Kelly."*

Kelly threatened to sue Mell and the alderman eventually recanted his claim of public sector jobs for sale. Blagojevich sought to make the best of this turn of events, boasting that it took "testicular virility" to support my landfill bill and take actions that protected the public even if they displeased his political patrons and family members.

But it was too late, the damage had been done. *Chicago Tribune* columnist John Kass described the fallout in retrospect:

> *"Once Blagojevich and Mell fell out, once they began fighting and blaming each other and airing the family's dirty laundry, once Mell publicly accused his son-in-law of corruption, it was over for Blagojevich. Without Mell guarding his flank, Illinois House Speaker Michael Madigan had no qualms about cutting [Blagojevich] down to size. Given that the governor's own father-in-law had accused his administration of selling jobs, the US Attorney was obliged to investigate. The clock was now ticking for Rod Blagojevich and it didn't look good."*

My landfill bill (SB 431) passed and was sent to the governor on 7/19/2005 and became Public Act 94-0272. It seemed almost anti-climactic after all the drama. The governor had hijacked my bill for his own purposes but that was nothing new—he did that to many pieces of legislation. Yet the legislation itself was a step forward in protecting the public from what had seemed an intractable problem of politically connected landfills that endangered public health and were largely immune from regulation. Frank Schmidt sold his ownership of the Will County landfill in 2008 and in July of 2011, he [Schmidt] plead guilty for evading $1.3 million in taxes on the sale of the land.

By 2005 my responsibilities as the Illinois Senate Majority Leader had grown more complex as I tried to keep the legislative agenda moving in the Senate at a time when the governor and Speaker Madigan were pulling in different directions.

I had been raising my children on my own at this time and I truly believed no man would put up with the schedule and commitments that I had not only as a legislator but as a leader in the state Senate. However, I was wrong about being forever single and as years went by my relationship with Jim blossomed and we were married in December of 2005. Meanwhile, the Blagojevich-Mell family had been torn into separate, hostile camps. Rod's wife Patti sided with her husband and refused to speak to her father. The two did not speak for several years until her mother became seriously ill. The depth of Mell's estrangement from the governor was such that he would come out in public support of the governor's Republican opponent Judy Barr Topinka in the 2006 election. When I was running for congress in 2008, Mell also showed some hostility toward me for my involvement in the landfill legislation by telling me he was supporting my Republican opponent. While I was not aware of his connections to the ownership of the Will County facility, it would not have affected my determination to protect residents from the consequences of illegal dumping. I am not someone to back down from something that is so vitally important.

Blagojevich's public spat with Mell fit nicely into Speaker Madigan's plans to block Blagojevich's legislative plans and any means of funding his programs. The governor's plan for universal health care was known as "Illinois Covered" and had attracted national attention from health care advocates but the price tag of $2.1 billion was a problem. Former US House Majority Leader Dick Gephardt who represented America's Agenda, a non-profit group advocating universal health care, made weekly trips to Illinois to meet with both Governor Blagojevich and Speaker Madigan to try and broker an agreement. Blagojevich made a number of concessions, reducing the price tag $1.2 billion but Madigan refused to budge, even when a group of representatives gathered in his office urging him to compromise. Madigan simply told legislators they could "do what they wanted to do" before turning back to the work at his desk.

Speaker Madigan's efforts to block any initiative by the governor presented a dilemma to those who saw a golden opportunity to expand health insurance coverage and improve education under a Democrat governor. As Senate President Emil Jones, Jr., put it, "The Speaker's bent on breaking the governor . . . starving the government of revenue. When you starve the government of revenue, it doesn't fall back on the lawmakers, it falls on the chief executive officer." Jones spoke for many others in the legislature when he suggested that the speaker's actions served his desire to make his daughter, Lisa, the next governor of Illinois. Madigan "wanted to make him [Blagojevich] look bad so that people would be upset with the governor—then he could bring his daughter in and run for governor . . . That's what it's all designed to do."

Obviously, there was no way to know Madigan's motivations for certain, because anyone who knew the speaker knows he's a man of very few words.

Blagojevich made the speaker's task that much easier by going his own way instead of developing a common strategy with those of us who had been working on expanding health care coverage all along. At one point the governor issued an executive order increasing the income eligibility from an annual income of $38,000 for a family of four to $82,000 which greatly expanded the program. Under state law such a change in existing provisions of a program would have to be approved by the legislature's Joint Committee on Administrative Rules (JCAR). When these changes were submitted, JCAR ruled that the expansion plan was illegal and had to be curtailed immediately. The Blagojevich administration, however, continued to sign up new enrollees despite the ruling. Whatever the merits of the health care expansion, which many legislators supported in principle, this governor's action was widely viewed as an abuse of power and it would eventually become one of the articles of impeachment against Blagojevich the following year.

Money Dictated Election Results

As the 2006 election approached, the governor and his fundraising committee put together an unprecedented war chest that was certain to drown out any Republican challenger, despite the storm clouds gathering in the form of US Attorney, Patrick Fitzgerald's, investigation "Operation Board Games." The Republicans had chosen Springfield veteran Judy Barr Topinka, a generally well liked state treasurer, who was the sacrificial lamb in Blagojevich's lavishly financed reelection campaign. Blagojevich, who had already raised $18 million before the Democrat primary overwhelmed his well regarded but underfunded Democrat primary opponent, Edwin Eisendrath, a former Chicago alderman and Housing & Urban Development (HUD) administrator. Eisendrath had campaigned against corruption in the Blagojevich administration, but public perceptions had not yet caught up to the reality of Blagojevich's modus operandi, which had become pay-to-play on steroids.

In a move that seemed well timed to damage Blagojevich's chances in the November general election against Topinka, US Attorney Fitzgerald announced the indictment of corrupt Blagojevich operatives Antoin "Tony" Rezko and Stuart Levine, charging they had extorted millions from individuals and companies seeking to do business with the Illinois Health Facilities Planning Board and the Teachers Retirement System (TRS). The two men were raising funds for "Official A" according to the indictments. A week later, Levine pleaded guilty to the charges and signed a plea agreement that identified Rezko and "Official B" as conspiring with him to extort campaign contributions in return for state business. Blagojevich was later identified as Official A and his top fundraiser, Chris Kelly, was identified as "Official B." It wasn't long before Kelly was found dead from an apparent overdose of pills and poison in Country Club Hills, Illinois.

Despite the exquisite timing of these indictments—just weeks before the election—they had little immediate impact. Regarding Tony Rezko, Blagojevich said, "If, in fact, these allegations relating to Tony are true, he betrayed my trust. He lied to me, he deceived me, and more important than that, he violated the public trust." Given later revelations about Blagojevich's direct involvement in these activities from a court ordered wiretap, the governor's statement seemed reckless as well as cynical. Surely the US Attorney would be putting very heavy pressure on Rezko to talk about the governor's participation in illegal fundraising schemes. Blagojevich seemed to be practically daring Rezko to talk as part of a plea agreement, because that was how the US Attorney built his corruption cases against public officials. When Fitzgerald investigated Governor Ryan his former chief of staff, Scott Fawell, reluctantly became a key witness against Ryan because, as he put it, Fitzgerald put his "head in a vice." Rezko had to have felt that vice too.

Republican gubernatorial candidate, Judy Barr Topinka, raised $11 million, a respectable sum for a governor's race in Illinois, but she could not begin to compete with Blagojevich's war chest of $27 million in 2006. Blagojevich's commercials seemed to take over television. The governor's advertisers had a field day when they discovered video of Topinka dancing the polka with the now disgraced former Governor George Ryan. They turned it into a TV commercial which seemed to run relentlessly.

"He [Blagojevich] had all this money," Topinka later complained. "He didn't have to leave his house—he could sit down and comb his hair and just run those commercials of me dancing with George Ryan. My polka with George Ryan didn't cost the state anything! It was just a dance. And that commercial was played all the time—making me look like George Ryan's love child. It was great advertising. It was great propaganda. He murdered me on that, because I could not fight back." Blagojevich ended up defeating Topinka by almost ten percentage point, in November of 2006, despite the indictments of two of his key fundraisers.

The Arrogance

It did not take long to see that Governor Blagojevich had an inflated view of himself that obscured his ability to grasp the reality of the forces displayed against him and his own ability to overcome them. His vanity was evident to all who dealt with him. An aide assigned to him carried a case that contained a fancy hairbrush known as "the football" a sort of comic counterpart to the nuclear code information package, also known as the "football" that accompanies a US President when he travels. In so far as Governor Blagojevich was able to accomplish at least some of his goals, much of the credit would go to his deputy governor Bradley Tusk, a well organized operative who had worked for New York Senator Schumer before joining the Blagojevich administration. In our regular day to day dealings, leaders of the General Assembly, including myself, dealt with Bradley Tusk rather than the governor. Tusk was only twenty-nine when he became deputy governor and took on many of the functions that a governor would normally handle. Blagojevich clearly hated spending time in Springfield, preferring to be in Chicago with his family in the leafy Ravenswood neighborhood of Chicago. Tusk was disgusted when Blagojevich asked him to hold up a $2 million grant for the Chicago Academy, a school in Congressman Emanuel's district unless Rahm's brother Ari, a Hollywood agent, held a fundraiser for the governor. Tusk considered it an unethical as well as illegal request and made sure the school received the grant and the fundraiser was never held but Tusk had had enough and returned to New York to oversee Mayor Bloomberg's reelection campaign.

The governor never lacked for big ideas, but was often at a loss how to accomplish his goals. He also nurtured the idea early in his first term, that he might have prospects as a presidential candidate. It is an idea that certainly seems ludicrous today, but his larger ambitions at least kept the governor engaged at the beginning of his administration while his deputy governor and the leadership of the Illinois Senate moved forward on legislative goals. By passing the *All Kids* insurance bill, Illinois became the first state to guarantee health insurance for all children. Illinois also became the first state to offer preschool for all three and four year-old children and in 2003 the bill I sponsored—a prescription drug program for senior citizens and people with disabilities also became the first of it's kind. The state's workforce was reduced by twenty percent during this period as well.

The governor's plans to expand services inevitably clashed with his pledge not to raise income taxes which were substantially lower in Illinois than adjoining states at the time. Even the governor's allies in the Senate quickly concluded that he was not a team player or one to share credit. The governor would hold press conferences on Sunday to announce initiatives or sign legislation that many others had helped create without inviting any key sponsors. Many of us felt he abused the amendatory veto to put his stamp on scores of bills, because he always had to portray himself as the hero. When we wanted to give a certain low income group of seniors free rides on public transportation, the governor sought to upstage us with an announcement that he was making free rides for *all* senior citizens without consulting members of the legislature who could have looked into the impact on the state budget.

A Very Unpopular Tax

As the cost of various services strained the state budget, and with the governor refusing to consider a modest income tax hike, he came up with the idea of a "gross receipts tax" on business transactions. Blagojevich did so without bringing key legislators on board. I remember President Jones holding a leadership meeting in downtown Chicago and inviting Governor Blagojevich into our meeting because he [governor] had this great idea that was going to "fix" everything. After hearing his explanation of the gross receipts tax I quickly piped up and said that it was a terrible idea and it wouldn't work. I was told otherwise and to watch it move through the legislature. Under my breath I was mouthing "Not with my vote." For now Senator Rickey (Hollywood) Hendon was still the governor's number one cheerleader and said if the governor was for it so was he, sight unseen. Soon business lobbyists had put together a major campaign against the gross receipts tax which included television advertising. Madigan saw a chance to embarrass the governor with a non-binding resolution opposing the gross receipts tax idea. Without defenders in place and with the tide overwhelmingly against passage, the governor finally called on his own supporters to vote against the resolution, which they eagerly did, resulting in a 107 to zero defeat for the measure. However, this did not happen before those of us on Senate Executive Committee (which is made up solely of Senate leadership) were pressured to vote on the measure to move it to the full Senate for discussion. There were quite a few bills that went to Senate Executive Committee so vulnerable members never had to vote on controversial pieces of legislation.

The Governor' Tardiness Always Present

As the 2006 election approached, Republicans were excited about their prospects of reclaiming the governor's mansion, but Blagojevich had been steadily raising record campaign funds despite a sharp decrease in his popularity. With tons of money to run and a lavish television campaign ready to roll it would not be the Republicans who would bring down Governor Blagojevich.

Nixon Story:

Not long after the election, a dinner was arranged for a group of legislators at the governor's mansion. Those of us in attendance were curious to see how the governor would handle the gathering given his strained relationships with not only his adversaries, but those who were presumed allies. Guests began arriving at the scheduled time but of course the governor was not on hand for his own dinner party. Finally, an hour-and-a-half later, Blagojevich arrived in his running attire all sweaty from his run. He excused himself to clean up and returned an hour later. Instead of using the occasion to smooth over frustrations and to develop better communications with legislative leaders, the governor launched into a bizarre and long winded story about an encounter he once had with Former President Richard Nixon. After graduating from Northwestern University, Blagojevich and a friend decided to visit New York. Blagojevich knew that Mr. Nixon went for a walk every day at the same time and decided to try to run into the former president by camping out near his home when Nixon took his regular walk through his Upper East Side neighborhood. The plan apparently worked and Nixon and the young governor-to-be had a conversation while Nixon gave autographs and posed for a picture. The governor's self absorption was evident throughout what remained of the dinner. There was little effort to repair communications with a group of legislators he needed to move his agenda forward. Blagojevich's obsession with Nixon though, was revealing. He identified with

Nixon's "me against the world" attitude and, like Nixon, saw himself very much as the besieged outsider, trying to do the right thing while maintaining a state of denial about his own very real shortcomings.

Demuzio Funeral:

The governor's tardiness was constantly on display. A very distasteful portrayal of this tardiness had occurred in 2004 when the he arrived late for the funeral of Illinois Senator Vince Demuzio, who died at sixty-two after a long and difficult battle with colon cancer. I can remember sitting in the church so long waiting for Blagojevich that the Lieutenant Governor, Pat Quinn, had to step in at the last minute to do the ceremonial state flag presentation. It wasn't until the funeral was almost over that Blagojevich sauntered into the church thinking everyone had waited for him.

Blagojevich Really Thought He Should Be the President

Some people believe Blagojevich's frustration had roots in his unrealistic belief that he could be taken seriously as a presidential candidate especially after seeing Barack Obama's meteoric rise as a national figure. Blagojevich did not lack for charisma or the ability to communicate with voters. Unfortunately, he was undisciplined about the nature of governing, unwilling to work as part of a team and unable to see how his own actions put himself and others at risk. On more than one occasion, the governor would be addressing a large audience and declare to them about a grant the group would be getting. I believe one of the groups was the Urban League and the grant was in excess of $1 million. By contrast, Obama was always well prepared and knew how to make strong allies to advance his agenda.

Blagojevich and his fundraisers were brazen in making pay-to-play the operating formula for state government. Over a six-year period, Blagojevich managed to amass a staggering $56 million for his campaign. In thirty years of politics as a legislator, secretary of state and governor, George Ryan, had only raised $40 million. In a 2008 story called the "the governor's $25,000 club" the *Chicago Tribune* found that 235 contributors had contributed the sum of $25,000 to the Blagojevich campaign and of these contributors, three quarters received either state contracts, appointments to state boards or favorable action on regulatory or policy issues. In return for this now standard size contribution, "a state lawmaker got a six-figure state job, one of more than four dozen donors awarded jobs or appointments by Blagojevich. One Chicago pharmacist previously told the Tribune—and law enforcement—that his $25,000 check to the governor's campaign was the price tag for fixing a critical state audit of his drugstore, an allegation the fundraiser who solicited the check adamantly denied."

The Down and Dirty Regarding the Ethics Bill

Although the public did not know the extent or details of these corrupt arrangements, those of us who had been pressing for strong ethics legislation felt that the publicity surrounding "Operation Board Games" investigation now gave us a very good chance to pass a bill to stop the sale of government contracts and appointments. There was a lot of back and forth between different committees and between the Senate and the House of Representatives over a three year period, but a very strong bill House Bill (HB) 864 was passed in May of 2008 that bans businesses and their owners with more than $50,000 in state contracts from making campaign contributions to the office holders awarding those contracts. This legislation also requires all state contractors to register with the State Board of Elections and to report all contributions made to political committees.

I may have been listed as one of the Senate sponsors of HB 864, but that barely describes the crucial role I had to play in order to get this bill to the floor of the Senate. There had been times I disagreed with the Senate President but this issue put me squarely up against him who as Senate President, continued to have a working relationship with Blagojevich at a time when others had given up. After both the House and Senate finally passed the bill in May of 2008, Governor Blagojevich used his amendatory veto to expand the legislation to apply the donation ban to lawmakers and included other items targeted at legislators' outside work and pay raises.

It was vintage Blagojevich, hoping to put the legislators in the position of having to explain why they were applying standards on contributions to state office holders that they would not accept for themselves. It was also clear that Blagojevich was using this tactic cynically to delay, kill or just take over as his own a bill that had wide support and dealt with a serious problem that the governor had made infinitely worse. The House of Representatives had overwhelmingly overridden Blagojevich's veto, but Emil Jones stated that he was not going to call the Senate into session until November, and that the fifteen-day rule requiring Senate action on the bill would not apply until then.

In September, Barack Obama, now a US Senator and presidential candidate, publicly called on Jones to bring the Illinois Senate back into session to deal with the Ethics Reform bill. Jones relented almost immediately, saying "I plan to call the Senate back into session to deal with the issue of ethics, only at the request of my friend Barack Obama. I still stand by our interpretation of the fifteen day rule."

From my vantage point as Chairman of the Rules Committee I was very frustrated that Emil was holding on to the ethics bill for the governor's benefit. Each day the Rules Committee would meet without the ethics bill getting the Senate Presidents' approval for release. This went on for months and frustration was mounting not only for myself and Senator Harmon, the sponsor but for the members of the Senate, both Democrats and Republicans who were constantly coming to me asking why no ethics bill was coming out of Rules.

The press was relentless, as were the Republicans in following my every move and making some kind of remark or comment once I was an announced candidate for congress. At one point I explained to everyone how flattered I was with all of the attention but sadly for them, not doing anything different than normal.

The only way to move the bill forward was to use my power as chairman of the Rules Committee to block all other legislation from going forward. I had warned the president many times that I wanted the ethics bill out of Committee. I found it somewhat hypocritical that Jones' method of leadership was to empower the chairmen to control their own committees but I guess the controlling part didn't include the Rules Committee. I was serious when I told him I would not convene another Rules Committee if I did not see the ethics bill on it. Sure enough, I guess he didn't believe me and I refused to call the next Committee meeting to order. Within minutes I received a visit from Jones' chief of staff (not the Senate President himself) who reminded me that I served as Chairman of the Rules Committee at the pleasure of the Senate President and that my position on the committee could be taken away as fast as it was given to me. I told her I understood how things worked around here but it didn't matter and I wanted the ethics bill out of Rules. If there was a problem I expected Emil to tell me himself, not to send another messenger. Obviously, I knew the likely consequences but the passage of the bill was more important to me at this point than being Chairman of this or any committee for that matter. I followed through on refusing to convene any more Rules Committees which then held up all bills from moving. Something was going to happen one way or another and I did eventually get my way on the ethics bill even if it did come out as a "shell". It not only cost me my chairmanship, I was removed from the committee altogether. It had become too much of a distraction on an issue that Jones didn't want to deal with. Distractions aside, HB 864 was now going to a full committee to be debated, changed, voted on by the full Senate to become law. Sometimes you need to stand up for what you believe in no matter what the consequence.

There are many affirmations and quotes that I have posted on my walls but a favorite of mine is: *A Successful Woman is One Who Can Build A Firm Foundation With The Bricks Others Have Thrown At Her*. I am still trying to figure out what the governor had over the Senate President that caused him to keep the ethics bill bottled up which he knew could hurt many of his members. The reason I have been able to help as many people and do as much as I have over my twenty years is because I had no PERSONAL agenda to get in my way. Those personal agendas have a tendency to cloud your judgement at times and I promised myself when I got involved in politics there was never going to be anything standing between me and doing the right thing. Things come along and then some people tell themselves that it would be okay "just this once." If you can compromise your values "just this once" it will be easy to compromise your values again. Meanwhile, the comprehensive ethics legislation played an important part in the governor's downfall.

The Governor Gets Arrested and the Pieces Fall Into Place

After my election to Congress a large group of us were having breakfast at the Democratic Club in Washington, DC, during new member orientation and I about broke my neck to get a look at the television set in another room to see Blagojevich who was being arrested at his home. He was charged with bribery, wire fraud, conspiracy, lying to federal authorities and other charges. It was December 9, 2008. The indictment, based on a court ordered wiretap of his office and home, made it clear that the governor had become especially reckless in conspiring to shake down important institutions (racetracks, a hospital, the *Chicago Tribune*) in order to collect as much campaign contributions as possible before the new year when the ethics bill would go into effect. This made it much easier for US Attorney, Patrick Fitzgerald to act. The rumor going around was Blagojevich happen to *say* he was ready to appoint Jesse Jackson, Jr. to the vacant US Senate seat now that he had all the commitment necessary to receive a minimum of $1 million in campaign cash for the appointment. Whether true or not, by just saying those words, it was enough for the US Attorney to move in because he couldn't take any chance at this point. It was a complete shock that the US Attorney decided to move in and make the arrest at this point but he had no choice having heard that Blagojevich was only days away from making his appointment to the vacant US Senate seat. "The government obtained information that Rod Blagojevich was accelerating his corrupt campaign activities to accumulate as much money as possible before the start of ethics legislation on January 1, 2009 that would severely curtail Rod Blagojevich's ability to raise money from individual and entities conducting business with the State of Illinois."

The most sensational charge was that Blagojevich and his aides were in effect seeking to *sell* the US Senate seat that Barack Obama had vacated to become president in return for possible financial favors or future appointments of Rod Blagojevich and his wife to prestigious, well paid positions, possibly even a cabinet position. In a profanity-laced conversation recorded on the wiretapped conversation with his deputy governor, Doug Scofield, Blagojevich discussed his power to appoint a US Senator: "I mean I, I've got this thing and it's f–g golden and I'm just not giving it up for f–g nothing."

The wiretaps showed that Blagojevich discussed potential appointees to the US Senate with Rahm Emanuel who then provided a list of five candidates that the White House felt would be acceptable including Obama's senior advisor Valerie Jarrett, but would not offer any favors to Blagojevich in return and the governor is heard on the tapes complaining bitterly about that.

The federal indictment referred to a "Senate Candidate 5" who was under consideration by Blagojevich, because there was some indication that either he or his representatives were willing to raise money for Blagojevich in return for an appointment by Blagojevich to the US Senate vacated by Barack Obama. Congressman

Jesse Jackson, Jr., acknowledged that he was "Senate Candidate 5" in the indictment, but strongly denied that he had authorized anyone to speak for him.

Fast forward more than three years to June 21, 2012, Raghu Nayak got indicted on federal charges that he bribed doctors to send patients to surgical centers that he owned. However, he is best known in Illinois for allegedly offering a bribe to Governor Blagojevich to purchase a US Senate seat for US Representative Jesse Jackson, Jr.

On June 22, 2012 Phil Kadner, a longtime columnist for the *Daily Southtown* wrote an article *"The Great Ragu's Stench and Illinois Politics"*. The column mentions the details of how Kadner remembers his discussion about all the gory details with Jackson. Kadner's column reveals that Jackson (D-2nd) once described Nayak as a sort of humorous blowhard, a self-important fellow who always had big plans but who nobody took seriously. Well he took him seriously enough when he asked Nayak to fly his mistress to Chicago. That was before Jackson told congressional investigators that Nayak was a friend who often visited his congressional office in Washington. Kadner also mentioned that if you trust a person to not tell your wife about your lady friend, I think you would trust him with just about anything. Whether or not a guilty verdict was returned both Jackson and Blagojevich surrounded themselves with slime balls. There is only one reason you do that, and it has nothing to do with good government. According to Kadner, Congressman Jackson continues to deny that he ever had anything to do with a bribe in exchange for a US Senate seat. The real problem is that Jesse chose Raghu to be his friend and confidant, his drinking buddy and his travel agent for his "social acquaintance". There are good, honest, hard-working elected officials and then there are those who are shady, dishonest characters who are willing to bend the law. Jackson, will tell you he has not been convicted of any wrong doing. Do you have to be "convicted" to have done wrong? You decide.

In 2009, the House Ethics Committee said it was investigating whether Jackson used public resources—in the form of his Chicago and Washington, DC, staff—to vie for the appointment to the Senate seat. US Attorney, Patrick Fitzgerald, asked that the House Ethics Committee delay their investigation until proceedings against Blagojevich had concluded. In December of 2011, after the US Attorney told the House Ethics Committee they were done with their investigations they voted to continue their investigation into Jesse Jackson, Jr., since the report US Attorney, Fitzgerald, handed the Ethics Committee mentioned a "probable cause" violation numerous times. According to the *Chicago Sun-Times,* the House Ethics Committee would be looking into reports that the two men who represented Jackson made specific offers of fundraising for the governor if he appointed Jackson to the US Senate seat. Rajinder Bedi, a state official, who claimed to be one of Jackson's representatives met with the governor's brother, Robert, in late October 2008. According to Robert Blagojevich, Bedi offered more than $1 million for the seat on Jackson's behalf. Bedi testified as a prosecution witness that he had met with Jackson earlier on the same day that he met with Robert Blagojevich and that both fund-raising and the Senate seat were discussed in Jackson's presence. Bedi also testified that when he passed along the offer, Robert Blagojevich turned it down. A second approach of the same offer was made [according to Robert Blagojevich's testimony] on Oct. 31, 2008.

Although my former Illinois Senate colleague, Barack Obama, was assembling his presidential staff and cabinet and I was getting my office in order as Congresswoman; Governor Blagojevich continued to insist that he would use his power to appoint a US Senator despite his upcoming impeachment proceedings in the Illinois legislature and his criminal conspiracy trial in US federal court. Warnings from Senate Majority Whip Dick Durbin from Illinois and Senate Majority Leader Harry Reid to Blagojevich that the US Senate would not seat anyone he appointed, did not prevent the governor from appointing former Illinois Attorney General Roland Burris as the US Senator to replace Barack Obama. Could the choice of Burris over Jackson, Jr., for the vacant US Senate seat have anything to do with Jackson not supporting Blagojevich for governor in his first primary?

What happened back in 2002 was Blagojevich had asked Jesse Jackson, Jr., to support him in the primary for governor and Jackson had promised that support. Blagojevich and Jackson had become friends while serving in Congress together but 2002 was the year Jackson rivals ran someone with the same name as Jackson on the ballot. Jackson's father, the Reverend Jesse Jackson, told him not to walk away from his African American roots [the African American candidate which happened to be Burris] in favor of a white man in the midst of what could be a difficult campaign for Jackson, Jr. who capitulated to the Reverend and pulled his support from Blagojevich in favor of Burris and Blagojevich never forgot that betrayal. Burris was a friendly African American politician from downstate Illinois whose career as state comptroller and attorney general proceeded without scandal, but whose ego and ambition blinded him from grasping that he had become a pawn in a power struggle between a disgraced governor and senior political leaders who wanted to distance themselves from all that he had come to represent. By appointing an African American politician as the successor to Barack Obama's US Senate seat Blagojevich hoped to forestall opposition to his choice, but Illinois Secretary of State, Jesse White, a popular African American leader who had been reelected by wide margins refused to sign a certificate of election validating the governor's selection of Burris.

The stalemate ended only after Durbin and Reid acknowledged they lacked a legal basis to prevent Burris from being seated.

It was Blagojevich's last political victory before the Illinois state Senate voted on January 29, 2009 to unanimously remove him from office. Senator Terry Link, who was first elected along with Barack Obama and myself spoke for many when he told the *Chicago Sun-Times* before the vote: "There's nothing happy about this. We're doing something that's going to be history forever. But I'm glad we're going to be opening another chapter in a few hours." Moments later, Lt. Governor Pat Quinn took over and replaced Blagojevich as governor. He served out the remainder of his term and was re-elected for a four year term in November, 2010.

7

Decision to Run For Congress

2008

House Speaker Nancy Pelosi did her best to persuade me to run for Congress but also respected the need for my husband, Jim, and myself to consider all the factors that would be going into this major decision. We went to Washington, DC, together in September, 2007 to talk to a number of people not only the Speaker. She was very gracious to open her home to us on a Sunday afternoon. We talked about my life, her life, kids, grandkids, about us both being Italian-American and anything else of interest. In the end she said: "Deborah, you have very important things you are doing in Illinois and many constituents who are depending on you. You also have a very important decision that only you and your family can make. I would love to have you run for Congress, but that is not my decision to make. When you decide, please let me know. After all, you are Italian-American. We are very strong women. Please let me know after you and Jim have had time to discuss this."

She impressed me as a very classy lady. That didn't mean I agreed with all her politics, but I respected her. She grew up like I did, basically with brothers, tough and not afraid to communicate with her male counterparts. Unlike me, she did come from a political family which gave her an advantage. She may not have been a darling in the women's movement because she rose through the political ranks as I did by being "one of the guys." Pelosi has shown her strength when it counted and has helped women candidates achieve success along the way.

Our next stop was Congressman Chris Van Hollen (D-MD). He pulled no punches. He explained what they were looking for. I had been recommended by Congressman Rahm Emanuel and others and he acknowledged if I were ever to run there was never a better time than now. He finished our conversation by putting in a little extra plug saying if I wasn't the candidate for this seat in congress they had no intention of spending money at all in this race. I am not sure if that was true but it may have been just the shove I needed because there was no way I was going to let this congressional seat go to a Republican without a fight. Congressman Jerry Weller (R-IL) had just announced he was not running again so it was now an open seat. I had been courted to run for congress several times before. In fact I still have a letter from Congressman Steny Hoyer (D-MD) thanking me for my consideration after I had made the same trip to Washington, DC, in 1999.

Jim and I went to one of our favorite restaurants, Capitol Grill, for dinner and started to assess the next step in our life. Once we made the decision to run for office there was no turning back and we put all our blood, sweat and tears into this race. I started raising money and putting a staff together.

I couldn't believe the amount of money that was needed to run for congress. Rahm liked to call me nearly every day to find out how much money I had in the bank. Congressman Emanuel believed the only important aspect of a campaign was money and that no one wants to give money to a candidate who doesn't already have a lot of it. One day I answered the phone brusquely and told him I didn't know I worked for him. He laughed and said, "You know, you are right. You don't." From then on he started calling me "boss" before asking me how much money I had in the bank.

I had offices all over the district filled with paid staff as well as volunteers and everyone worked around the clock. I didn't mind being on the phone all the time asking people for money but I sure missed walking door to door and having interaction with the voters. It was hard to teach an old dog new tricks as I frequently tried to sneak out of the office to hit the streets with walk sheets only to be pulled back to the phones. I was told that things were different now and commercials communicated with the voters. Commercials cost money, the money I needed to raise. I got pretty good at it and raised several million dollars. Once I proved to everyone I could raise money and I was going to win I was then put on the *coveted lists* that candidates would die to get on. Money arrived every day by UPS, US mail, FedEx and in person. We were producing commercials, sending out mail and knocking on every every door six times.

Mayor Tim Balderman of New Lennox who won the Republican primary and the right to be my opponent in the general election dropped out shortly afterward because of his frustration that his party leaders were now asking him for his Christmas card list to raise money from. He hadn't realized there wasn't outside money available to pay for his campaign. He was eventually replaced with Marty Ozinga a concrete company owner. He was the perfect opponent because as it turned out he had given Blagojevich a $10,000 campaign contribution and was heard on TV saying "Very few Americans don't have health care. If you get sick you go to the ER, that is what hospitals are for." The Republicans sure didn't pick him because he was politically astute but he could fund his own campaign and his name was on every cement truck so he had great name ID. I also had a very capable Green Party opponent, Jason Wallace. The three of us appeared together at forums and debated regularly around the district.

The 11th Congressional District spanned eight counties and was made up of urban, exurban as well as rural areas. It also included Illinois State University, Governors State University and Illinois Wesleyan University. Turnout amongst young people was expected to be at an all time high because of the Obama excitement.

I was elected as the Congresswoman of the 11th Congressional District in 2008 (which I won 58% to 34% against Marty Ozinga Jason. Wallace received 8% of the vote).

Throughout 2008 from the time I made my decision to run until the time I took office in January of 2009 the nation was transfixed by the Democratic nomination battle between Barack Obama and Hillary Clinton and then the battle for the White House with presidential candidate and Republican nominee, Senator John McCain. There was also the increasingly perilous economic situation with the sub-prime mortgage meltdown that reached a crescendo with the bankruptcy of Lehman Brothers in September of 2008. After eight years of the Bush administration people were ready for Obama's message of hope and change.

In December of 2009 as I was about to resign from the Illinois state Senate in preparation for my term in the US House of Representatives, Jesse Jackson Jr.'s (D-IL) name surfaced as US Attorney, Patrick Fitzgerald, arrested Illinois Governor Rod Blagojevich at his home for a variety of pay-to-play offenses including the alleged selling of the US Senate seat left vacant when Barack Obama was elected President the previous month. Governor Blagojevich who had the right to appoint a US Senator to fill the vacancy was caught on tape offering the position to a number of potential candidates in return for substantial campaign contributions and other benefits to the governor. The press quickly learned that the one candidate who appeared ready to engage in such discussions, identified by the US Attorney as "Senate Candidate Number 5," was in fact Jesse Jackson, Jr. He thereafter came under a cloud as a result of the events that eventually led to Blagojevich's removal from office and subsequent conviction on a number of felonies related to the pay-to-play shakedowns in return for political contributions and other favors. As this book is being written, Congressman Jackson still continues to be investigated by the House Ethics Committee for many things including using government dollars for political purposes and has been on a medical leave for months with no indication of when he will return.

Freshman Orientation

Senator Dick Durbin (D-IL) had been extremely helpful during my election and I deeply appreciated his allowing me to set up a temporary working office inside his Senate office.

Orientation for new members was hosted by then Majority Leader Steny Hoyer (D-MD) who served at the time in the number two spot under Speaker of the House Nancy Pelosi (D-CA). We were told things by a number of speakers for several days. Among those that stood out were:

- since the beginning of this country to 2008, less than 10,000 people had served in congress, less than three hundred of them women.
- new members were advised that anything in writing even an email can be considered public and end up on the front page of a newspaper.
- told about the strict ethic rules
- security and terrorists issues were talked about

We were given escape hoods and told that the Capitol police will let us know when we need to put it on. The escape hoods would protect us from radiation or other chemical or biological attacks.

Majority Leader Steny Hoyer (D-MD) talked about the need for consensus. Representative John Larson (D-CT) said to never forget the people back home because they are the reason you are here. Representative Chris Van Hollen (D-MD) Chairman of the Democratic Congressional Campaign Committee (DCCC), noted that only two Democratic incumbents had lost in 2008 and one of them refused DCCC help. Majority Whip Jim Clyburn (D-SC) spoke about solidifying the middle of the Democratic spectrum. He was talking about us. Most of the newly elected Democrats were from districts that leaned Republican. However, many of them as well as independents felt disconnected from the last eight years of the Bush administration. Representative Clyburn was serious when he said not to lean to one extreme or the other because we now had eighty-one Democratic House members elected in 2006 and 2008 from districts where former President George Bush previously won. What that meant to me was these districts felt disenfranchised like my husband, Jim, and no longer voted the party line. Representative George Miller (D-CA) said you will want to save the world, but save your seat first.

We received so much advice on the first day our heads were spinning and it would not take long until we would soon find out that any playbook people were reading from would have to be thrown out the window because little did we know what we were soon going to be up against. There had never been anything like the 111th Congress and the subsequent election we were about to experience in 2010.

Our days were now a blur of orientations, hiring of staff, renting office space back in the district and finding a place to live in Washington, DC. Congressional offices were selected during orientation based on seniority. There were more than fifty incoming freshman in 2009 from both parties. We were brought together in one rom for the all-important lottery for picking offices. My lottery number was terrible [fifty-one] but we were fortunate one of our top picks was still available. It was located on the fifth floor of Longworth tucked into a side hallway. We hallway. We changed the colors of the curtains, carpets and the paint on the walls so the office was new and clean to us. It was home and we loved it there. It seemed the perfect location; we were close to everything being in the Longworth office building. When I walked into my office for the first time I noticed a large safe taking up a good amount of valuable shelf space. I didn't think anything about it but knew I didn't need it and had it removed. I recently read a book by Congressman Robert Wexler (D-FL), *Fire-Breathing Liberal* who mentioned a story about a safe he found in his office. He explained in his book [p. 47] that before the first campaign finance laws were passed political contributions were routinely made in cash. The amount of the contribution was determined by the importance of the member. A senior member on a good committee could bring in as much as $10,000 in one day. Members didn't want to leave that kind of money lying around and needed somewhere to keep all that cash so they put it in the safe. If that story is even remotely true it looks like money has been influencing politics and politicians for a long time.

I arrived in Washington with a few projects I set out to accomplish. One of them was to transform the soon to be closed Silver Cross Hospital in Joliet into a veterans' mega clinic. I quickly sought out to find out exactly what I needed to do and who I needed to see. I didn't see the need to wait until I was sworn in.

The Pride of Being an American and The Work That Needed to be Done

Anyone who aspires to become a member of Congress and feels a deep sense of pride in being an American is sure to feel a surge of adrenaline walking through the hallowed halls of the US Capitol and entering the historic House chamber as a newly elected US Representative. I certainly did. I also strongly felt the hopes of millions of citizens raised by the election of America's first African-American President. He was someone I knew personally and believed had the intellectual qualities and temperament to successfully grapple with the daunting economic, social and foreign policy challenges that Americans faced in January of 2009. Whether four years in the US Senate was enough national experience to move his agenda forward would soon be tested. The stock market and the job market were in free fall since the previous July and millions were out of work with more to follow. Meanwhile American soldiers were being sent home seriously injured from Afghanistan and Iraq conflicts that seemed to have no end.

When I was elected to the US House of Representatives I believed naively that I would be doing more of what I did in the state legislature just on a bigger scale. I couldn't have been more wrong. Congress is its own world. It's different on every level; a different pace, different intensity, and different stakes. This was a blood sport not for the faint of heart.

There was a cascade of events that foreshadowed the exhilarating and turbulent first two years of the Obama administration.

Drinking Out of A Fire Hose

The question I was asked more than any other was: what surprised you most when you got to Congress? The answer was easy—almost everything surprised me. Washington, DC, was very different from Springfield.

The reality is that your Congressional representative is your direct connection to the federal government. The House of Representatives was established by the founding fathers to be directly responsive to the beliefs and needs of citizens. US Senators are elected to six year terms and if there is a vacancy, can be appointed by a governor. Vacancies in the House, however, take far longer to fill. The Constitution requires that a member of the House be replaced only by an election held in the congressional district of the former representative. According to the US Constitution and state law, the governor of the state calls for a special election to replace the vacant House seat. The full election-cycle must be followed including political party nominating processes, primary elections and a general election, all held in the congressional district involved. The entire process often takes as long as three to six months. Members of Congress must answer to the people at all times because election year is always around the corner. Although all 435 seats in Congress are up for reelection every two years, most folks don't know that less than seventy-five of them are ever competitive. The others face no or minimal opposition and continue to serve year after year until they decide to retire.

The pace of activity for members during the 111th Congress was said to be like "drinking out of a fire hose" a phrase coined by Congressman Ron Klein (D-FL) who was defeated in 2010 by Tea Party favorite Allen West. The endless rounds of committee hearings, votes, constituent visits, caucuses, fundraising and press calls were unlike anything else I experienced in the Illinois General Assembly which met several days a week for a little more than five months out of the year. Congress seemed to always be in session and when it wasn't I traveled back to the district on the weekends to meet with constituents. I was determined to be visible and active from the very start. When you are one of 435 you can't just sit in your office watching the debate on the TV monitor or in the back row of committee, you have to step up and be part of the debate. On January 21, just a few weeks into the new session I was already presiding over special orders. By the end of the two-year session I was presented with the *Golden Gavel* by Speaker Pelosi for the most time presiding over the business of the House of Representatives as a freshman member of the House. Along with my award came a letter from the Speaker that read,

Dear Representative Halvorson,

Many thanks for your hard work and dedication to the role of Speaker Pro Tempore. Your fresh energy and management of many hours of debate and voting on the floor of the US House of Representatives are greatly appreciated.

Please accept this gavel, used to preside over the US House of Representatives in the 111th Congress, as a small token of my appreciation for your work and service. Thank you for your leadership and friendship.

best regards, Nancy Pelosi

One of the members I spent time with on the floor was Representative Patrick Kennedy (D-RI). He showed me the flashcards his staff made for him of the incoming freshmen representatives with pictures on the front and names on the back so he could familiarize himself with those of us who were just elected. I thought it was such a great idea that I asked my staff to do likewise for the entire membership of the House and that is how I learned everyone's name. I knew that it mattered very little that you were on record "for" something or "against" some project or policy. You had to do the work, stay focused and be prepared to be in people's faces about the issues that mattered, whether it was a particular bill or funding for a project like high speed rail, the Veterans Mega Clinic at Silver Cross, or the big Will County inter-modal facility. I spent my entire first term getting to know my district and the people who lived in it. I did everything I was told a new member needed to do to be successful and every evening after dark when I was leaving my office I stopped to look at the Capitol dome to pinch myself at how fortunate I was to have the honor to serve. To all who aspire to serve as a member of Congress don't let a day go by without looking at the Capitol dome on the way out of your office each evening to thank God and your constituents for the wonderful opportunity to serve your country.

2010

I Had an Opponent Three Days After I Was Sworn Into Office

The speed at which all this was taking place was breathtaking. I was surprised to find out that only three days after I took the oath of office in 2009, my future election opponent [Adam Kinzinger] with the help of the Illinois Republican State Party Chairman was already putting out press releases criticizing me. It was a tactic apparently planned and used in other districts across the country before the new administration even took office. Could such a formidable opposition have been mobilized so quickly on the national level if Obama were not an African American? Not likely because this well-financed Republican political operation was in place with their marching orders before President Obama had taken a single action as President. The upcoming 2010 election would prove to be a national referendum on anyone who had a "D" after their name.

Traditionally voters wait to see what actions a newly elected official takes over time, how they respond to events, what accomplishments they achieve and whether they keep their word to the voters. The opposition typically waits to pounce on an

elected official until they make mistakes or break promises and vo
policies. I was not alone. This was well-orchestrated across the cou
of us had a chance to do anything good or bad. This was hyper-
steroids and it arrived in opposition to Barack Obama and the Demo ontrolled
congress that forever shredded the modicum of civility. Increasingly it had become a blood sport. It didn't matter what you did, how hard you worked, or how you voted. Those of us who lost in 2010 didn't all have the same voting record. It didn't matter, nothing mattered.

As a state Senator I looked forward to parades in my district as an opportunity to see and be seen by my constituents but after the Tea Party fight against the health care bill as a member of Congress I felt like I was running a gauntlet. Walking with my daughter, Stephanie, in a parade in one small town which had always been a friendly place I heard angry taunts, "Don't come near me," and "You traitor, get out of town." Many were obscene and ugly. Anti-choice groups waved babies in my face, yelling, "See what you kill!" One of my opponent's campaign operatives began to walk alongside Stephanie and me, yelling out to those watching the parade, "She is a liar, here's proof," while passing out false literature.

Whether he was aware of it or even cared, my opponent Adam Kinzinger's staffer and his cohorts were spoiling the parade for everyone including the children watching and turned it into a display of incivility. Stephanie had grown up surrounded by rough and tumble Illinois politics and she regularly talks about the time in 1996 when she and her brother were watching TV in our home and a brick was hurled through the window of the room they were in. Tied to the brick was an intimidating note that I should get out of the race. Neither she nor I had ever experienced such hostile and angry behavior that made people so vile they would do whatever it took to hurt whoever got in their way. I continued walking determined not to be intimidated. I would ask God daily where was this hatred for not only me but for others like me coming from. To get through this period I fortified myself with daily meditation and prayer and reading inspirational messages on five by seven cards during quiet moments of my workday and taking comfort in the teachings of Christianity. I kept these notecards in my car, in my desk and anywhere else I could think of to have them at my disposal ready to read since it did help to get me through some really rough days and some were tougher than others. It is one thing to be able to debate the issues and stand up for what you believe in and then there is another thing to stand up to protect yourself from the outright evil and hatred that seemed to come out of nowhere.

Running for reelection was different. No one could have predicted the fallout of the Tea Party and the racial divide when it comes to having an African American President. Is it any different with regards to a woman in a leadership position? Have we really come a long way? Or have we now gone backwards? If you ask me, it just means we have to work harder to keep moving forward. Change takes time. We can't give up. I have many favorite sayings and another is "Progress always involves risk. You can't steal second base and keep your foot on first."

Women in Politics

Dina Titus (D-NV) and Ann Kirkpatrick (D-AZ) were already talking about running for Congress again. I was so happy to hear there were women ready to go again because we really needed women like them back in Congress. The only thing I knew, it was too early for me to make a decision like that. I didn't even know what our districts were going to look like until the legislature passed a new map.

Women need to step up to the challenge and all of us who have learned how to overcome obstacles and fight for a share of power are going to have to redouble our efforts and share them with the next generation of women climbing the political ladder. In fact more women are running for office than ever before. The 2012 Project, a national nonpartisan campaign sponsored by the Center for Women in Politics that was formed in response to the unprecedented drop in women lawmakers after the 2010 election, has been encouraging and supporting women candidates of both parties in their bids to run for office. Now they are pleased to see their work pay off, as 110 Democratic women and 44 Republican women candidates for the US House of Representatives have won their primaries.

If you don't do politics, politics will be done to you and women have become complacent from the work of generations before.

Most believe the loss of so many women in the 2010 election was a backlash against House Speaker Nancy Pelosi. Everywhere I went people would tell me how much they despised her. One of my opponent's commercials used my words calling her a "classy lady" against me. As I campaigned in my rural district I saw pick up trucks with big wooden signs that read: "fire Pelosi, dump Debbie".

Women can't be afraid to stand up, take risks and to support issues of special concern to them. Those of us who plan to seek political power can do it but it sure helps when you have support at home. There are many men who are uncomfortable with strong women like my first husband. I recall a gathering of congresswomen who, like me had begun as state legislators and within the first two years each of us had been divorced. Most of us were now remarried to supportive husbands. Jim and I work closely to maintain a family life that accommodates our busy schedules and provides quality time each other.

I could not have imagined doing my work as a member of Congress without him. We were a team doing everything together and sometimes he had to be my surrogate in another part of the district. I know I have talked about my husband, Jim, in other chapters but it is important to mention how much he gave up to be my partner and support me to represent the people and work hard as a congresswoman. He shared me with more than 700,000 people. He was alone at home while I was gone four and five days a week in Washington, DC, and he was attacked through the social media and in person by people who did not believe in my policies. Jim lost friends and he lost customers because he could not sit idly by and ignore the many comments sent to him. He would do his homework, find out the truth and respond back with the source. I tried to tell him to ignore it that people didn't want the truth but that wasn't Jim. He believed people needed to be informed. The email that got to Jim the most was "members of Congress serve just one term in Congress and get free health care and a pension for the rest of their life." If that was the case why would anyone ever run for a second term.

During lame duck session, Leader Pelosi asked me if Senator Durbin and Illinois Governor Quinn had gotten together with me about a job. She was concerned because I was one member she didn't contemplate losing. I told her I would be fine. I don't blame her for pulling money out of my race because Rep. Van Hollen and Rep. Debbie Wasserman Schultz had tough decisions to make. There is only so much money to go around and there were many times I was reminded that I had won by twenty-four percent in 2008, I didn't need as much help as the others. What I am bitter about was that those of us who were elected in 2008 from swing districts knew what was happening back in our districts and were not taken seriously. We were just told they needed our votes and not to worry about it because they would be there for us when we had to run for reelection but they were not there for us. I don't think all the money in the world could have saved us. So the election of 2010 proved Rahm Emanuel wrong when he preached that money was the most important thing in elections. If you don't have a message, all the money in the world isn't going to help and the message slipped through our fingers like sand. All the great things we were able to accomplish and no one could come up with a cohesive message? It was incredible. I will never forget when Mark Zandi, Chief Economist for Moody's Analytics and a one-time McCain advisor, would visit our caucus and tell us he was amazed that we were not getting credit for all the great things we were able to accomplish with regards to the economy.

Representative Shelley Berkley (D-NV) graciously opened her home in DC so all the Democrat women could get together one last time to share the stories of what we accomplished together. Chellie Pingree (D-ME) was the only freshman woman who survived the 2010 elections. The rest of us lost in 2010 and we were already making plans to get together. There wasn't a dry eye in the house by the time Speaker Pelosi spoke of our accomplishments together. The Speaker told me she turned to the president in my case and he told her he would take personal responsibility for my race but even the president couldn't save the districts like mine where it was a bad year to be a Democrat.

I took some time to do absolutely nothing and Jim and I went on a much needed vacation. When we returned, I started going through my twenty years worth of journals so I could begin writing my book. I had never read any of them and couldn't believe how overwhelming it became but I was determined to write my book. I sure am glad I kept a journal for several reasons. The details would be helpful for the book but journaling was so important for not only my emotional health but my physical health.

We always wanted dogs so by July we got a Boxer that our granddaughter named T-Bone and within five months another Boxer named Kokomo. It was also a joyous time to spend so much time with our grandchildren who were now able to spend weeks at a time at our house.

Between writing my book and spending time on my Government Relations Company, Solutions Unlimited, I was pretty busy. It was the first time in many years that I hadn't lived in two different places.

I was happy thinking I had closed the book on my ever running for elected office. At least that is what I thought . . .

8

The Health Care Bill That Almost Wasn't

Living at risk is jumping off the cliff and building your wings on the way down.
—Ray Bradbury

During the first two years of the Obama administration the majority of what came out of Washington was the discourse regarding the health care bill. You would have thought nothing else was accomplished and unfortunately the Democrat's message was lost along the way. The House had actually passed their version of a comprehensive health care bill quickly, but it was blocked in the Senate and then bogged down with fruitless negotiations and messy deals to gain votes that only tainted a process already ladened with misinformation.

Republicans stayed relentlessly on message that the health care bill was "budget busting" and "job killing." These were false claims for anyone who bothered to read the nonpartisan Congressional Budget Office (CBO) analysis which estimated the *Patient Protection and Affordable Care Act* would expand coverage to thirty-two million uninsured Americans at a cost of almost $1 trillion over the next decade and cut the deficit by $138 billion over the same period through new fees, taxes and cost saving measures. Asked about this finding, Republican leaders simply said they didn't believe it though these same leaders were always quick to cite the respected CBO when it served their interests. Passing a health care bill was no small accomplishment given many unsuccessful efforts going back far as Theodore Roosevelt. Harry Truman, Richard Nixon and Bill Clinton all had tried and failed. For the first time preexisting conditions could not be used to deny health care coverage and seniors would be able to afford prescriptions that were previously unaffordable for many because of the "donut hole."

Explaining What No One Wanted to Know

Two of the issues I was actively involved in—relief to small businesses and preventive health care—were measures that could save both costs and lives. How sad that during such a historic moment we couldn't even go home with a message that would resonate with our constituents. Those of us in the freshman class begged the Speaker and all of leadership to do a better job of getting the message together about this health care bill because it wasn't striking a chord back home. Every week we were told to be patient and do a better job of explaining it to our constituents. Those of us who had just won elections in swing districts knew that one member of Congress was not going to be able to get a message out to people who had already made up their minds based on misinformation. It was going to take an all-out effort by the president to use the national base that had just overwhelmingly elected him. Instead he left the leadership of the health care negotiations to Speaker Pelosi and Congress.

Republicans Dominated the Message

Unfortunately, as we had predicted the battle over health care legislation played out in agonizing fashion in the first year of the Obama administration and allowed Republicans to dominate the media message with simplistic slogans repeated till we were all nauseated. This changed the momentum of the Obama presidency in the critical first year and allowed Republicans to threaten to filibuster bill after bill in the Senate simply by picking up a wavering Blue Dog Democrat. Other key initiatives like the energy and jobs bills were stalled as Republicans gained confidence and were able to double down on their strategy of denying President Obama anything that might improve the economy before the 2010 midterm elections. The way the health care strategy was handled and the long delays gave rise to the Tea Party which then put the Republican focus on the budget deficit rather than creating jobs.

No Leadership

On those occasions, when I spoke with the president in private or in public I raised the issue of his administration losing the message on health care. It didn't matter what we talked about, the conversation always ended with, "Don't worry, Debbie, my poll numbers in your district are still very high. I will be there for you during your reelection." I told him that it wasn't about reelection it was about what we needed to get done now. I was the one that went back to the district on the weekends and things were not good. Again he would tell me not to worry. More often, I found myself voicing this concern at Speaker Pelosi's weekly Wednesday morning meetings she held with freshman members. The Speaker always brought plenty of staff members along with her to answer any questions and we were advised by staff members to continue holding meetings with different constituent groups to get their input on the ever evolving bill. Our freshman class was made up of talented men and women who were ready to add to any unified message had there been one. Leadership members either didn't return to their home districts like we did or they didn't have to contend with what we we were encountering from Tea Party zealots and constituents deluged with Republican sound bites.

There was much speculation in the press about why Obama, who had shown his talents as a gifted communicator throughout the election seemed to keep above the fray and let Congress fight it out amongst themselves on the health care issue. We all believed his leadership on this issue would have made the passage of the health care bill go much more smoothly. Given Rahm Emanuel's reputation as a strategist there were questions about why the White House had not put together a campaign style effort on behalf of the health care bill. To my knowledge this puzzling strategy has never been explained publicly and probably never will; but I believe that differences between the President and his Chief of Staff, Rahm Emanuel, over administration priorities had the effect of cancelling each other out. Rahm Emanuel was known to have opposed tackling the health care issue early on in the new administration, perhaps still thinking about how the Clinton administration tripped over this issue in its first term. Emanuel felt that the primary focus needed to be jobs and the economy, but President Obama believed that he could walk and chew gum at the same time so pursuing both issues were necessary and politically expedient as his political capital was sure to wither as the recession ran its course. As a result, the White House only sporadically joined the debate while Republicans and their Tea Party supporters seized the opportunity to define "Obamacare" as they wished.

The Polls

Having convinced those who were predisposed to believe that the *Affordable Care Act* was a "socialist" attempt at a big government takeover of health care and would institute "death panels" as Sarah Palin warned, the Republican strategy now portrayed the administration as forcing the enactment of legislation that no one wanted. Polls on the subject of health care legislation, however, were inconclusive. They found that a significant number of those who opposed the legislation felt that it did not go far enough because it did not include a public option as an alternative to the private insurance system. When these individuals were added to those who supported the *Affordable Care Act,* they formed a majority in favor of comprehensive health care legislation.

I Wanted A Bill That Worked—Robust Public Option Not It

During our weekly caucus meetings there were discussions of what should be in the health care bill. The Progressive Caucus said it should have a public option that was tied to medicaid rates. There also was discussion that there should not be a public option at all. Without the public option the progressives argued this bill would only be a windfall for the insurance companies. So discussion started on a way to have a public option but tie it to negotiated rates. I knew tying anything to medicaid would not work because of my experiences with the program in Illinois: *All Kids*. You can create any kind of program you want but if there is no doctor to take care of you, giving someone a false sense of security of having health care is just wrong. The Progressive Caucus still wanted a vote on the health care bill containing a public option that was tied to medicaid rates. Speaker Pelosi had done her own count of the Representatives on a public option bill only to find the votes were not there.

I Wanted Results—Not Ideological Skirmishes

As someone interested in practical results rather than ideological skirmishes, my experiences with the Illinois *All Kids* bill led me to question the way the public option was being shaped. It is one thing to pass legislation like the *All Kids* bill guaranteeing access to health care for every child in Illinois, but it was another thing to find physicians who were willing to provide services at the low reimbursement rates that were offered. For a public option to work it would have to guarantee that physicians would be available to provide the services. I favored a system somewhat like those in place at Mayo and the Cleveland Clinic, where physicians are paid a fixed salary that is not linked to patient volume or income from fee-for-service payments. However, I was quick to mention that a one-size-fits-all system is not the answer either. It would take some time to find the right mix to end the wasteful practices of ordering expensive but sometimes unnecessary tests and instead reward good physician care. Not surprisingly this proposal was opposed by powerful physicians groups. I was an original sponsor of bills that banned insurance companies from denying children care because of preexisting conditions. I also was the sponsor of the healthy lifestyle discount signed into law that creates workplace wellness grant programs to encourage healthy living through counseling and seminars.

Lobbying Efforts

Whenever the big issues came up; people, organizations, lobbyist, unions and corporations would attempt to meet with me or our office to voice their opinions. Those who couldn't make it to Washington would call or find me at home on the weekends. Once I announced I supported health care reform but would not be supporting a public option tied to medicaid rates the phones started ringing off the hook. My interns could not keep up with all the calls. Every union leader and progressive group started calling thinking they could change my mind and many of these groups criticized and threatened my stance. I went home on Friday, October 23, with about fifteen to twenty calls I needed to make.

Emotions Were At An All-Time High

The Grundy County Democrat Chair, who was a huge supporter of mine cornered me at an event to tell me how disappointed she was in me and if I didn't vote for the health care bill with the *robust* public option in it she would not be supporting me for reelection. First I told her to calm down and then I told her I supported health care and we would eventually get a bill.

The emotions were at an all time high and it was very unfortunate that at a time when we could have been standing together, Democrats were eating their own. People were just doing what they were told to do—beat up on their congressman without knowing any of the facts. The unions who were calling me were basically saying the same thing.

The next morning I started on my long list of calls to return and they were all the same. Someone had told them to call me because they heard I was against the health care bill. I spent the entire day letting everyone know I was for health care but there was not a bill ready to be voted on; it was still evolving. The robust public option was never going to come to a vote because the votes were not there.

I had a long heated discussion that morning with Mike Carrigan the Illinois President of the AFL-CIO who I have a great relationship with. He told me "You need to support the *robust* public option because I got a call from the International Union President that you are being difficult." I thought *difficult*. Hmmm. So that's what it's called when you don't just roll over and become a rubber stamp for a group. Mike told me he was being pressured to unleash all his union members on me. I said, "Michael, I told you before where I stood and I am not caving to pressure just because you are getting heat from higher up." I asked him why he couldn't stand up for me knowing that I have a twelve year track record of being there and doing the right thing for the working men and women of the 11th District as well as Illinois and in the end we would have a good bill for health care. I wanted a bill that was going to work and this was not it. I told him and anyone else that would listen to me that there was no way enough votes would be rounded up for that bill. "Be patient, we will get a health care bill," I said to him. He repeated his threat of "unleashing" his members on me and I told him he had to do what he had to do. I really do not know where they were coming from to think that this kind of demeanor or pressure was actually going to get me to change my mind. I spent my entire weekend on the phone explaining my support for health care and fielding calls that wouldn't have been necessary if there was leadership from the top on the issue.

The health care bill with the *robust* public option never did get enough votes to be called for a vote just like I told all the people I talked to even though none of them wanted to listen or believe me.

Perception Becomes Reality in Many Cases

On one of my weekends home I was in Morris, Illinois, at the Corn Festival and I ran into one of the Shorewood Trustees, Lee Starr. Lee was relentless in his opinion that the health care bill would give healthcare to illegal aliens. He was vehemently opposed to the whole bill but especially the illegal alien part. When I attended events that were crowded such as this parade there were always so many people circling around me and this day was no exception. I was telling Mr. Starr what was in the bill and he was having nothing to do with the truth and when his wife came over to join him he lunged at me as if ready to attack; spit spraying from his mouth. I got out of his way just in time. I realized that people like Lee had become so angry from all the misinformation that was being distributed that it had become impossible to reason with anyone who disagreed with me on this issue. The reason I bring this episode up is because it was not an isolated incident. I had office hours in my Peru office one Saturday and people came in to complain about the health care bill or whatever was last reported on conservative radio or TV. As I listened to one middle-aged couple, they were so angry at me they got up, called me a bobble-headed bitch and stormed out. I think they were angry that I refused to engage in their their name calling. I had decided there were some people you could not make happy no matter what and all you could do was give them your time and listen. It was such a shame that these debates were so miserable that no one really wanted to know what was in the bill or be civil. The anger had become unbearable.

My District Travels and Stories

I knew we were in trouble when my staff and I mistakenly thought we were visiting a friendly crowd at a county health department and there were only two employees who supported the health care bill. We spent more than an hour at this facility listening to all of the reasons they did not like the bill. Somehow it was okay that they all had full benefits from the government but no one else should.

Then there were my *Congress on your Corner* events, the individual office hours I held all over the district particularly the one I had in the western end of my district. One gentleman (Warren) wouldn't even sit down. It was almost as if he sat down he would forget the talking points he had been rehearsing for days that he had heard on Fox News. One thing did throw him off. It was my husband, Jim, who was sitting in the meeting with me. Warren lost his train of thought for a moment when he demanded to know who Jim was and why he was in the room with me as spit was spraying all over me and the table. I calmly asked him to take his seat and he refused. His hands were planted on the table in front of me as he leaned over. Jim later said that he was worried about this guy jumping over the table at me but remained unruffled only because I was amazingly calm. It was a tense ten minutes while Warren ranted about all the things that angered him.

Since I am talking about *Congress on Your Corner* events it brings me to that awful event on January 8, 2011, just five days after the new 112th Congress convened. My friend and colleague Congresswoman Gabby Giffords was a victim of a shooting near Tucson, Arizona, which was reported to be an assassination attempt on her life. It happened at a supermarket where she was holding a *Congress on Your Corner* event. She was critically injured by a gunshot wound to the head; thirteen people were injured and six others were killed in the shooting, among them conservative federal judge John Roll. I found out about it like many others while watching the news on that Saturday morning. I was paralyzed for what I thought was forever; all I could do was sob. Our freshman class had been very close and when most of us lost our elections in 2010 Representative Kathy Dahlkamper of Pennsylvania put an email list together so we could keep in touch which we did often. Just them my iPhone went off indicating emails were coming in. Sure enough it was my colleagues. We were comforting each other for the next six or so hours as the news streamed in. At one point depending on what channel you were watching they reported she had passed away. I didn't think I could cry any harder but I did. Giffords was later brought to a rehabilitation facility in Houston, Texas, where she recovered some of her ability to walk, speak, read and write. Jared Lee Loughner, twenty-two was quickly arrested. He had been fixated on Giffords and handwritten notes were written by Loughner indicating his assassination plans. Federal prosecutors filed five charges against him, including the attempted assassination of a member of Congress and the assassination of a federal judge. The motive for the shooting remains unclear; Loughner did not cooperate with authorities invoking his right to remain silent. Loughner was found to be incompetent to stand trial based on two medical evaluations.

There were a number of times I had been in the company of Gabby when she voiced her concerns of how volatile things had gotten especially with regards to the immigration issue. Other Representatives who held town hall meetings in states where guns were allowed told us their horror stories.

In my district I found that medical providers who understood the *Affordable Care Act,* usually favored the majority of it. I met with two hospitals in Kankakee County. One served a range of people from different income groups and was very supportive of the bill. By contrast, the other hospital that catered to an upper income clientele seemed unaware of the many provisions of the bill and just wanted to strongly oppose comprehensive health care legislation claiming it was a "free ride" that would open the door for low income patients to flood their emergency room. It all came down to a willingness to accept the basic premise of fairness.

The Upcoming Health Care Vote

I happened to walk into my DC office one morning just a few days before the vote on the health care bill and there sat the Illinois President of the AFL-CIO Michael Carrigan and his Secretary/Treasurer, Tim Drea waiting to see me. It had been two weeks since our last [unpleasant] conversation. As it turned out we did get a health care bill as I promised, but it was not the public option they wanted. I didn't know what they were there to see me about but I figured I would soon find out. My labor legislative staffer, Justin, brought Mr. Carrigan and Mr. Drea into my office. I couldn't help but chuckle when they said they came to see the Illinois delegation and wanted to start the morning out with their "friends" first. There was something that bothered me and I let Mr. Carrigan know I didn't like being disrespected. Michael said it was something he had to do, getting the call from higher up. It would be different if we didn't have a long history of legislative accomplishments together. I had been with them ninety-nine percent of the time over my twelve years in the Illinois state Senate. During our heated discussion, Mr. Carrigan turned to Justin and said, "don't you have to go make phone calls or anything?" I said, "No, he doesn't. He is my liaison with labor and he will sit in on this meeting." Eventually, there were apologies and hugs all around because this was a confrontation that needed to happen. Too many times women allow themselves to be treated and talked to in a way to avoid confrontation. If you allow yourself to be bullied it will continue to happen. Standing up for yourself may not easy but if you don't do it you will never be respected. When handling these kinds of confrontations make sure they do not turn personal, stay professional, as was my experience on this day.

The Big Vote Passed, But Not Quietly—November 7, 2009

My apartment was ten *blocks* south of the Capitol on New Jersey Avenue, but on November 7, I might as well have lived ten *miles* away. The President was coming to Capitol Hill to talk about the *Patient Protection and Affordable Care Act* (health care bill) and most of the streets were blocked off. The fact that we were making history today may not seem like a big deal to some, but it was a huge deal around the Capitol Hill Complex. The morning started out with a few procedural votes and then the trouble began. Normally things happen "without objection" or with "unanimous consent" but today was not a normal day. So when the women Democrat Representatives decided to form a long line by one of the microphones to add a unanimous consent statement about the health care bill to the Congressional Record a Republican male Representative would yell "objection" which is all that was needed to stop discussion from going into the Congressional Record. This went on for quite some time until the Republican men figured out they were making quite a spectacle of themselves on television objecting to the Democrat women who were attempting to speak on a bill. Someone must of made some calls because within minutes a few Republican women started appearing on the floor to do the men's dirty work. One by one, the Republican women took over for the men yelling "objection" every time a Democrat woman tried to speak. It was a real shame to later hear the comments by people who had tuned into C-Span about what they thought of the spectacle that was made by members of Congress who were supposed to be adults.

President Speaks to Us

Around eleven o'clock in the morning all the Democrats went to the Cannon caucus room to listen to the President speak. It took less than a half hour for him to thank us for our leadership and to talk about what this historic day was going to mean to so many people of this country. As I sat there I couldn't help but think that it would have gone even quicker and smoother had the President stood in front of this caucus months ago leading the discussion and keeping the Democrats together with his enthusiasm and popularity, but hindsight is always twenty twenty. While we were all grateful that we had gotten to this day the liberals in the caucus felt the moderates may have won the battle but not the war. The divisiveness caused by a health care bill with no public option is something the Progressive Caucus was never going to get over. Their disdain for the moderates was worse than ever. Unfortunately, when more than fifty of the moderates lost in the midterm elections it wasn't the moderates who lost the war, it was the progressives because they ended up in the minority.

The anti-choice groups were busily putting together their amendments. Representative Bart Stupak (D-WI) and other anti-choice Democrats were working with him on an amendment so they could in good conscious vote for the health care bill.

Congressman John Dingell (D-MI) had for the last four hours been presiding over the dialogue on the health care *Rule* that would set the procedure and legislative template of the full debate of the Patient *Protection and Affordable Care Act* that informally became known as Obamacare. As he returned to his seat the congressman received a standing ovation for all the work he had done on health care over his many years in Congress.

On a normal day, you would never find the House Chamber packed like it was because there is always too much going on—committee hearing, meetings in offices, phone calls, call time and other constituent work. But today was not a normal day. The chamber was full of guests in the gallery and members filled the seats as they readied themselves for a long day. Representative Patrick Kennedy (D-RI) gave an emotional plea on behalf of his father US Senator Ted Kennedy who worked for many years on health care before he died and wished he could have been there for the vote.

Returned to My Office to Check in

At about 4:30 in the afternoon I went back to my office to check in with staff to see who was calling and to find out what they were saying. Three out of every four calls were not even from my district but those that were from my area were running about fifty-fifty for and against the bill. The complaints against the bill ranged from this is a government takeover, massive tax increase, veterans are going to lose their tricare, to you will go to jail if you don't buy insurance. Those who were for the bill said please vote for it I have a preexisting condition and can't get health care, my child was born with a debilitating disease and she is five now and our lifetime cap is already used up and other stories like that.

I Did Some Reflecting on Health Care Journey

It had been a hectic day and I needed some time to think about what we were about to do. I went into my office and closed my door, something I didn't do very often. When I did that my staff knew I didn't want to be bothered. I wanted to be alone with my own thoughts about the vote I was about to take and the history we were about to make. I had worked hard to find consensus, to find the truth and to do what was right. I wasn't a rubber stamp for anyone and didn't just roll over and give my vote on something this important. I was still battered and bruised but for a good cause. I thought about all the people I had met and what a wonderful experience it had been; bruises and all. Where else but America do you get an experience like I have had to listen to so many people, agree and disagree but at the end of the day make my own decision of what I felt was in the best interest of not only my district but the entire country. I thought about Emily from Bourbonnais who's skull is too small for her brain and when she lost her job, she lost her insurance and try as she might no one would insure her again. She received a lot of thank-you-for-applying-but-sorry-we-can't-help-you-letters. There was Janet from Ottowa with stage four breast cancer. She cannot get taken care of close to home. She has to drive forty-seven miles away to get her treatments. I thought about Yvonne of Shorewood who was diagnosed with Crohn's disease at eighteen and can't get insurance. Every time she ends up in the hospital it is more than $19,000 out of her pocket. There were many more stories of people I was thinking about like the small children who have chronic diseases who by the age of five have used up all the insurance they will ever have. That is called a life-time cap on insurance. I also went back and thought about all the constituents who told me they were against a health care bill because this wasn't their problem and it wasn't the government's either. What made me more determined than ever was thinking about the Frankfort and New Lennox parades in my district listening to the yelling of "I hope you have your resume ready, you are going to need it when we kick you out of office." and "You traitor, get out of our town." If it turned out that I would need to get my resume ready for casting a vote for a bill that I believed would not only be the right thing to do, but would truly keep people healthy and bring down costs, so be it. As far as being called a traitor: which means *someone who betrays a friend, country or principle*. They were not talking to me. You can't betray anyone when you do what you say you are going to do. Just then the pager went off indicating it was time to vote.

Enough Votes are Finally Secured

At about seven o'clock we heard the whip operation had finally secured the 218 votes needed to pass the bill so voting would commence soon. Between seven o'clock and eleven o'clock when the bill was finally called there were a number of individual bills and procedural maneuvers mainly from the Republicans in hopes of stopping or better yet, killing the bill. However when discussion was finished and there was nothing more to say they just called for the vote. The final vote was 220 to 217. Thirty-seven Democrats voted no. Clapping and hugging went on for what seemed forever. Those who had copies of the bill were going around getting signatures. All I wanted to do was get back to my office to celebrate with my staff who had worked hard on this bill. I made a quick round of congratulatory hugs and handshakes and sure enough as I walked into my office just shy of midnight they were all there waiting for me; not one of them went home. They had watched the debate on the office TV and waited for me to get back to my office to get all the details and be there to enjoy that moment of history none of us would forget.

Final Version of the *Patient Protection and Affordable Care Act* Passed

The Senate didn't pass their version of the *Patient Protection and Affordable Care Act* until the last minute on December 24, 2009. Between November 7, 2009 and December 24, 2009 all the wheeling and dealing in the back rooms to get the bill done was enough to make a person sick. Whether it was Ben Nelson's (D-NB) Cornhuskers Kickback of $100 million in extra medicaid funding for Nebraska, Senator Mary Landrieu's (D-LA) Louisiana Purchase for $300 million, Senator Menendez (D-NJ) for $1 billion in research subsidies for New Jersey, Senator Dodd (D-CT) for $100 million for a new hospitals in Connecticut or more money for new hospitals in North and South Dakota, Montana and Wyoming. These sort of examples are what taint this process. The President announced that all deals would be taken out when the bill reached Conference Committee. The health care bill was then sent to Conference Committee so the differences between the two bills could be hammered out between the House and the Senate. The final bill was passed on March 21, 2010, and Obama signed it two days later.

You would think once the health care bill finally passed and signed into law we could finally move on to the jobs bills but that didn't happen. The Republicans were more confident than ever that Obama would be a one-term president. They made sure that nothing more got accomplished before the midterm elections and prepared themselves to take over Congress.

Once the individual states started suing over the health care bill it was a domino effect. The Supreme Court finally agreed to hear the arguments on the legislation whether the individual mandate was constitutional or not amongst other things in the bill.

It took until June 28, 2012 when the Supreme Court upheld the majority of the law ruling the mandate was a tax not a fine and therefore fell under Congress' taxing authority. The Supreme Court did prevent the Federal Government from withholding all medicaid funds to states who fail to comply with the expansion of medicaid but rather only permitted the federal government to withhold new medicaid funding to non-compliant states. What made this so significant was the deciding vote was made by Chief Justice Roberts who almost everyone thought would have voted with the other conservative judges.

The Republican-controlled House of Representatives has voted to repeal the *Patient Protection and Affordable Care Act* not just once but thirty-three times since it received President Obama's signature in March 2010. Many did not expect the bill to be upheld, nor did they expect Chief Justice Roberts to side with the court's liberal wing. But now that it has passed many are asking are all these repeals worth it? Where could this possibly go this year? Democrats and other supporters of the bill are calling the move a political charade since the law has no chance of being repealed as long as Democrats control the Senate and the White House.

John Boehner (R-OH) Speaker of the House of Representatives had this to say the day before the ruling, "We've made it pretty clear and I'll make it clear one more time: If the court does not strike down the entire law, the House will move to repeal what's left of it." He continued, claiming, "Obamacare is driving up the cost of health care and making it harder for small businesses to hire new workers." Yes, this does send a clear message that no matter what the odds, or how long it takes, we are going to stand for the justice and liberty of Americans. It's clear and it's bold and it's exactly the stance we need.

9

111th Congress, Uncivil Wars

"If we're able to stop Obama on this [health care bill] it will be his Waterloo."

—Senator JimDemint, R-South Carolina

"The single most important thing we want to achieve is for President Obama to be a one-term president."

—Mitch McConell Senate Minority Leader

So Many Different Kinds of Democrats—We Are The Big Tent Party

Along the political spectrum there were different caucuses which members chose to identify with. The Blue Dog Coalition was a powerful group who identified themselves as moderates from Republican leaning districts who often crossed the aisle to work with Republicans to get a compromise on legislation. Their only stated policy position was that of fiscal conservatism. Many of them had been recruited by Rahm Emanuel when he was the Chairman of the DCCC and sought out military veterans and other traditionally conservative types to run as Democratic congressional candidates in marginal or Republican districts.

The Progressive Caucus is the liberal caucus who promoted issues such as single payer health care and had little patience with the other caucuses especially the Blue Dogs who strayed from the party line. Jan Schakowsky with the Illinois delegation did a great job articulating for the group as did Congresswoman Lynn Woolsey of California.

I was a member of the New Democratic Coalition that was born out of the Democratic Leadership Council (DLC). The New Democrat Coalition took moderate or liberal positions on social issues but had a more moderate and pro business position on economic issues. Their aims were to revitalize and strengthen the Democratic party; and believed in order to have a healthy economy we needed strong small businesses. A dynamic woman and mentor of mine, Representative Ellen Tauscher of California was the Chairwoman of the New Dems. President Obama told us he identified himself as a New Dem and occasionally invited our group to join him at the White House to discuss issues facing the country. Representative Tauscher left in June, 2009, to work at the State Department as the Under Secretary of State for Arms Control and International Security for Secretary of State Hillary Clinton. Congressman Joe Crowley of New York ably took her place as Chairman.

Then there was the Congressional Black Caucus whose membership was exclusive to African Americans. The caucus described its goals as "positively influencing the course of events pertinent to African-Americans and others of similar experience and situation" and "achieving greater equity for persons of African descent in the design and content of domestic and international programs and services."

There also was the Hispanic Caucus and the Asian American Caucus.

Everyone had their opinion heard and had a place because Democrats were known as the "big tent" party. Congressman James Clyburn who was the Whip did a fabulous job of keeping all the caucuses with each other yet independent because he understood the need to bring everyone together at the end of the day on legislation and most thought he was a magician. Maybe it was because he fed everyone once a week at the whip breakfast prior to the Democrat Caucus meeting. Food always brought us all together. During debates of big issues the Caucus met more often: several times a day if necessary. Democratic leadership did a great job keeping those who attended the caucuses informed. Of course not everyone would go but attendance was taken and Speaker Pelosi was known for the notes she kept. Many times in those caucus meetings things got a bit heated when the Progressives and the Blue Dogs debated the different sides of an issue. You could hear the most liberal Democrats complain that the moderate Democrats weren't really Democrats. However, when the Democrats lost the majority in 2010, it was because members of the Blue Dogs and New Dems lost their races. I imagine those members who questioned the loyalty of the Blue Dogs wish they were in the Democrat Caucus now. [At least many of them could be counted on for the one vote that mattered, the Speaker of the House.] The fact is, by now what is left of the Democrat Caucus hopefully realizes there are not enough Progressive-only districts in this country to hold on to a Democratic majority. What I appreciated about the Democrats was our caucus looked liked the diversity of our country and the majority of the time there was respect for each other's differences.

I know Senator Durbin wouldn't mind me telling a funny story about being asked by newly appointed Senator Roland Burris where the government housing was for Senators? Burris almost had a heart attack when he was told that members had to arrange for their own housing and also pay for it themselves.

Whatever costs we incurred in Washington were ours personally. Given this fact, and the constant need to return to the district each weekend it was not surprising that at least two members of our delegation—Mike Quigley and Dan Lipinski—slept in their congressional offices.

At a White House social event just a few months after President Obama took office he seemed tired and a bit distracted. However, as the President greeted me it was like seeing a piece of home for Michelle and him. As we all hugged they wanted to make sure I said hello to our mutual friends back home when I made my weekly sojourns back to Illinois–11. I think the group hug was an unspoken "Can you really believe we're here!" moment. The President posed for a picture with my stepson Jay who serves in the Army Special Forces and was wearing his dress blues. Future White House events, however, involved increasingly onerous security and we had to show our identification at a minimum of four different checkpoints after Michaele and Tariq Salahi, a socialite couple featured in a reality show, were revealed as gate crashers at a formal dinner for the Prime Minister of India.

Steering and Policy Committee Responsibilities

Because of my background in Illinois legislative leadership, Nancy Pelosi chose me to be on the all-powerful Steering and Policy Committee which maps out legislative goals and determines committee assignments. It was an honor and a good beginning for my term in Congress.

Having been picked for the Steering and Policy Committee I had an inside track on committee assignments and plans for dealing with health care, job bills and transportation bills that were important to the Illinois-11. Because of my stepson Jay's experiences I wanted to do all that I could to see that we took care of our veterans, particularly the thousands who suffered from terrible physical and psychological wounds. Regardless of ones feelings about the US involvement in Iraq and Afghanistan, everyone should be willing to see that the men and women we send to fight overseas should have the resources they needed to get an education, a job and affordable medical care.

I served as the freshman class president and I was appointed to the Veteran Affairs and Agriculture Committees. I also managed to get a waiver to serve on a third committee—the Small Business Committee. I was on two sub-committees which met regularly. This in itself surprised me because in the Illinois legislature, if something was assigned to a sub-committee, it essentially meant death for that bill. Since I was unable to secure a position on the Transportation and Infrastructure Committee, Congressman Oberstar, who was Chairman made me an *honorary* member of the committee and helped advance several of my transportation projects. He understood that many highway, railway, waterways went through my district.

One of the tougher votes we faced as incoming members of the Steering and Policy Committee, was the critical choice of chairman of the Energy and Commerce Committee which was held in the previous congress by the eighty-two year old Dean of the House [longest serving member of Congress] Congressman John Dingell of Michigan who was being challenged by California Congressman Henry Waxman. Dingell was one of the earliest proponents of national health care and had a long distinguished career, but with comprehensive energy legislation dealing with global warming coming up many environmentalists felt he was too solicitous of industry's opposition to regulation and some were concerned about how he might deal with the provisions on climate change and other controversial issues. Representative Waxman, by contrast, was widely admired by environmentalists, but opposed by industry, particularly the struggling automakers. I realized later the energy bill would be a priority for Speaker Pelosi and she wanted to remove every obstacle possible.

Passions ran high before the vote and there was a lot of pressure on members by supporters of both sides. I didn't indicate which way I was leaning, but a representative from Illinois who was also on the Steering and Policy committee pulled me aside as I was walking into the meeting to tell me that the only reason I was appointed to this committee was to be a vote for Waxman and that Representative George Miller, California, was in charge of counting votes. In any case, I did not believe that to be true or maybe I just didn't want to think it could be true. I was told by the more senior members that this was the first time they had seen a senior member about to be ousted from their committee chairmanship like this. When Representative Rangel voluntarily gave up his chairmanship of the Ways and Means Committee while the House Ethics Committee continued their investigation of him, Congressman Stark of California was next in line for the chairmanship but it was given to Congressman Sander Levin. Nothing ever stays private in politics and it didn't take long to hear that Stark was passed over for Levin because Levin would have been much easier "to handle" by the Speaker. The Steering and Policy Committee votes regarding committee assignments were usually perfunctory and the caucus usually rubber stamped the advice of this powerful committee. However, the vote that would take place in caucus after the Steering and Policy committee vote for Representative Waxman was close. Representative Waxman ended up winning by a 137 to 122 over Representative Dingell during the secret ballot vote of the House Democratic Conference and it caused quite a few hurt feelings.

Who Was in Charge of the Message and How Did it Get Lost?

Working together with the new president I expected the White House to craft a strategy that would take advantage of the Democratic majorities in the House and

Senate and move legislation forward without delay. This was crucial because whatever optimistic predictions about the economy the administration might put forward, most economists expected that the deepest recession since the Great Depression of the 1930s would mean high unemployment for quite some time. Therefore, time was in short supply to pass important legislation to improve the economy. I told many in the Obama administration that his political capital was going to vanish if the Democrats lost the House in 2010. The White House staff thought it would be next to impossible to lose the House and they told me so every time I had a conversation with them, but my colleagues and I were the ones who went back to the district in Illinois every weekend and understood how the people outside of Washington, DC, really felt. I didn't get a chance to fall in love with my own press releases like those working in the White House did.

Even with Democratic majorities in the House and the Senate it is hard to believe that getting things done was much tougher than anyone ever thought. The House did it's job and passed President Obama's jobs agenda but once the legislation made it to the Senate it seemed to die a quick death. This is what happened to the *American Clean Energy and Securities Act* that passed the House and was never brought to the Senate floor for a vote. In fact there were many bills that passed the House that were never heard in the Senate.

I believe President Obama wanted to pass health care before passing an energy bill but Speaker Pelosi opted instead to pass the energy bill. In fact during some of the private conversations I had with the president he mentioned as much to me asking me to help get the energy bill out of the House so we could focus on health care. I told him the energy bill was not ready and I remember him agreeing with me only to say it had to go first. Speaker Pelosi has since admitted in a television interview with Melissa Harris-Perry of MSNBC, that passing health care may not have been the most politically expedient thing to do [possibly referring to losing the House] but that it was the *right* thing to do. I am proud of my vote on the *Patient Protection and Affordable Care Act* and wouldn't have changed a thing.

People have argued and asked why Congress doesn't listen to the voters? But voters rarely speak in unison. This country is evenly divided on almost everything. I was elected in 2008 when access to health care and high gas prices were the top two issues. How ironic that when Congress passed legislation to address both issues dozens of members were voted out of office because of it.

While in the Illinois state Senate a group of legislators from the South Suburbs of Chicago formed the Southland Caucus which included House and Senate members, Democrats and Republicans. I was it's first chairman and we became a force to be reckoned with because we worked closely together on transportation, education and other issues that benefited the South Suburban region. We could argue and disagree all day long on pieces of legislation but we put our individual differences aside and worked together on the big issues because there wasn't a Democratic road or a Republican bridge, they were everyone's roads and bridges-infrastructure for all Americans to drive on. It was very frustrating to watch how in Congress they would rather things fail than negotiate. Everything has become so partisan that compromise seems to indicate weakness.

Negotiate and compromise have become bad words but it is exactly what we need to get this country back on the right track. No more of this my way or the highway stuff. The red districts are just getting redder and the blue districts are getting bluer because the elections aren't in the fall anymore, they are in the primaries and the candidates are being forced to move as far to the extreme as possible which only hurts our country.

State of the Union

Congressman Joe Wilson of South Carolina received national attention when he interrupted a State of the Union speech President Obama was giving to a joint session of Congress by shouting "You Lie!" I was stunned. Congressmen Gary Peters, Kurt Schrader and I were speechless as we looked at each other then tried to figure out who said it. The looks on Speaker Pelosi and Vice President Biden's faces, who were seated behind the President, were priceless.

What the President said to bring about this outburst was, "There are those who claim our reform efforts will insure illegal immigrants. This too is false. The reforms I'm proposing would not apply to those who are here illegally . . .

That is when, in a breach of decorum, Representative Wilson pointed at Obama and yelled the infamous, "You Lie!" Those in the balcony who added to the unfortunate display were taken away and the president didn't skip a beat.

The congressman was inaccurate because HR 3200 expressly excludes undocumented aliens from receiving government subsidized "affordability credits." The nonpartisan Congressional Research Service agreed that people would need to be lawfully present to be eligible for the credits. However, undocumented aliens would have to buy their own insurance coverage through the Health Insurance Exchange. After the State of the Union speech the Obama administration noted that in the final bill, illegals *cannot* participate in the exchange. To show how sad this lack of civility really is: in the week after the speech Wilson raised $1.8 million in campaign contributions. The National Republican Congressional Campaign described him as their fundraising star.

Illinois Delegation and our Own Polarization

As the partisan rancor grew in Congress the Illinois delegation began to mirror the same problems. Normally, as a bipartisan group, we sought out issues where the benefits to the state were clear to both parties. *Sun-Times* columnist Lynn Sweet told me that when former Republican Congressman Denny Hastert served as Speaker and hosted the bipartisan delegation meetings, there was little controversy, despite the fact that Democrats were deeply opposed to Bush policies.

Senator Durbin carried on from Congressman Denny Hastert's monthly meetings of the Illinois delegation lunches. We had terrific guest speakers depending on who was in town like Governor Quinn or Mayor R. Daley. Given the near unanimous Republican hostility to the agenda that Obama had been elected to carry out, it was not surprising that Illinois delegation meetings would begin to reflect that, especially when the Obama administration began to study the vacant Thomson "super-max" Correctional Center in northwest Illinois as a place to house terrorism suspects that had been detained at the US military base in Guantanamo, Cuba.

Republican leaders were determined that Obama would not be able to close Guantanamo prison which was used to incarcerate terror suspects that were picked up en masse in the early days following the 9-11 attacks on the World Trade Center and the Pentagon in 2001. Some of these prisoners were guilty of aiding al-Qaeda in heinous crimes, but it also became clear that others were simply in the wrong place at the wrong time and had been swept up by US forces and intelligence operatives. At the US base in Guantanamo, Cuba, these prisoners languished for years on end without being charged with a crime. Whatever Americans thought about this abuse of our system of law, Guantanamo was seen around the world as a blot on our reputation and it became a recruiting tool for al-Qaeda.

Finding a place to incarcerate terrorism suspects was not easy and other countries with fewer resources were reluctant to take them. Except for congressional politics, the Thomson Correctional Center built at the former Savanna Army Depot appeared to be ideal to accept one or two hundred prisoners. No prisoner had ever escaped from a US super-max facility and the Federal Bureau of Prisons was set to build a new security fence that would exceed super-max standards. The nearby town of Thomson which had suffered with the recession was highly receptive to boosting local employment. Local law enforcement organizations were strongly in favor of moving forward on this project. This was not enough, however, for the Republican members of the delegation, particularly Representative Don Manzullo who represented the area. Manzullo, who once called Islam a "savage religion" was given to long winded harangues when the delegation met that sharpened the political difference at a time when we needed to band together on projects good for the state of Illinois. Increasingly Manzullo was joined in his efforts of obstruction to use Thomson prison by Representative Peter Roskum and Senator Mark Kirk.

Kirk had gained a reputation as a moderate Republican representing the wealthier suburbs north of Chicago. He had voted for the energy bill the previous year, but was now running for the US Senate against some Tea Party backed candidates in the Republican primary so of course he said that vote was a mistake and sounded increasingly truculent in his positions, clashing angrily with US Senator Durbin and was being disruptive of our common agenda wherever he could. Representative Judy Biggert (R-IL) was also known for being a moderate and then her voting changed. Representative Schakowsky (D-IL) confronted her one day about her change in voting pattern and she acknowledged she was fearful of getting a Tea Party challenge during the next primary.

I did not accept any of the arguments either for or against using the Thomson Center without checking first hand. I wanted to see Thomson Correctional Center and on a Sunday my staff and I went to visit the site of the correctional facility. The security features we saw were impressive and the prison itself was located in an isolated area that appeared ideal for the purposes of incarcerating terrorism suspects in a way that was consistent with American ideals and the law.

I didn't stop there and arranged for a briefing by the Department of Defense which would be in charge of the former Guantanamo inmates at the Thomson Center under Obama's plan. The Bureau of Prisons would be in charge of the rest of the facility. As the briefing concluded I asked the Department of Defense (DOD) what other members of our delegation had been briefed and was told that I was the only one. The same unclassified briefing I received was thereafter given to the Illinois delegation along with a positive assessment by the sheriff's police representing the area, but the Republicans, led by Representatives Manzullo and Kirk stayed on the attack, with Manzullo harshly criticizing the representative of the Sheriff's police for supposedly "not doing his homework" on Homeland Security.

At this point I hit back, pointing out that the Homeland Security Department had done the research and that the sheriff's department had done theirs. I pointedly thanked their representative and told him to go back to the sheriffs and chiefs of police and thank them for their efforts. Not another word was said at that point. Later, Representative Mark Kirk asked for his own private classified briefing with Department of Defense [DOD]. Durbin, who was the senior Illinois Senator and held the number two position in the Senate, said that he should also be there. Disgusted with the tone of the meeting, Representative Jan Schakowsky had already walked out, but those who remained were shocked when Representative Kirk (R-IL) refused. He feared that Durbin would share his classified briefing with Alexi Gianoulias, the Democratic Senate candidate Kirk expected to run against in the fall to fill the seat Senator Burris was keeping warm. Representative Hare (D-IL), said "no way, Senator Durbin needs to be there." As of this printing, many inmates at Guantanamo continue to be held without concrete charges, but until the wars are over it is thought that Guantanamo is still a haven for terrorists and many even if innocent have no place to go. There are no countries willing to take them. Congress has repeatedly refused to close Guantanamo to this day.

10

Healing the Wounds of War

Take sides. Neutrality helps the oppressor, never the victim
Elie Wiesel

Regardless of your position on the conflicts in Iraq and Afghanistan, all members of Congress could agree that our soldiers who had sacrificed so much in their service to our country needed support as they reentered civilian society. Many were returning with grievous wounds both visible and unseen. They needed jobs, understanding, housing, educational opportunities and long term medical and psychological care. In many cases their spouses needed training and support as caregivers. As obvious as these needs may seem my family's experiences with Jay and other wounded veterans we met indicated that there would be much work to do for the incoming Obama administration and Congress to make the system work better for veterans.

A Parent's Almost Worst Nightmare

It was a middle-of-the-night phone call that my husband Jim and I received in August 2008 that brought the war in Afghanistan home to us personally. We learned that our son, Jay, had been seriously injured in Afghanistan and was being flown to a hospital in Germany. That was all the information we had. Jim was pacing about and I was searching on the Internet "Where do injured soldiers go in Germany?" We deduced that Jay had been sent to Landstuhl Medical Center. In the morning I left a message on Illinois Congressman Phil Hare's (D-IL) cell phone. Congressman Hare was a well-respected member of Congress who replaced

Congressman Lane Evans in 2007 having been a long-time aide of Evans'. Hare served on the Veteran's Affairs Committee and was known as a veterans expert. I had my Illinois Senate staff put together a statement in case anyone found out what happened; and, to keep it short because I didn't want this politicized.

That night Will County Executive Larry Walsh and State Comptroller Dan Hynes were holding a fund raiser for my congressional campaign. As hard as it was, I had to say something about Jay so my supporters would not be upset if they heard it somewhere else first. There was not a dry eye in the room as I described what had happened. The fact that we knew so little may have made it worse simply because the unknown holds greater fear.

Then an amazing thing happened the next morning. Jim got a call from Congressman Hare who stunned both of us by saying he had just seen Jay. "You couldn't have seen Jay," Jim said in disbelief. "Jay is in a hospital in Germany." Phil said, "So was I and I got to visit him in his room." Jim was astounded. Congressman Hare explained that he had been on a congressional delegation trip to the Middle East and stopped at Landstuhl Medical Center in Germany on the way back to the United States. During their tour, a doctor said to Phil, knowing he was from Illinois, "We just received a young man from Illinois, would you like to visit him?" Congressman Hare said, "Of course," and went right in. It happened to be Jay! The reason Phil knew he was our son is because he introduced himself as a Congressman from Illinois and Jay said, "You must know my step-mom, she is running for Congress: Debbie Halvorson." Phil Hare about fainted and said, "You have got to be kidding me. Of course I know Debbie and she is going to win."

What a small world. Phil told Jim that Jay was talking and seemed to be in good spirits for what he had been through which made both of us feel much better. Jim also found out that Jay would not be having his surgery in Germany, they were preparing him to head out to Walter Reed Hospital in Washington, DC. Jay had broken his neck (C4) and his nose when he fell about twenty-five feet off a bridge answering a call to help another group during a fire fight. It was dark and the terrain was rugged. He was a Captain in the Army Special Forces and was the Commander of a fire base on the Afghanistan/Pakistan boarder. He later received the Bronze Star for this action.

Word travels fast because it didn't take but a few hours before I received a call from the Speaker of the House, Nancy Pelosi. She called to see how Jay was doing and to make sure Jim and I were okay. She asked if there was anything she could do and said she was praying for all of us. Jim finally talked to Jay. He was in a lot of pain and not too talkative. One of the liaisons that Jim talked to said Jay would be having surgery soon and would be in a brace for eight weeks. Congressman Rahm Emanuel (D-IL) called to see how we were doing, as did Senator Dick Durbin (D-IL) and Illinois Veterans Affairs Director Tammy Duckworth. Tammy wanted us to know that she spent a lot of time at Walter Reed after she lost her legs in a helicopter crash while serving in Iraq. She told us to call if we needed anything.

Jay was transferred to Walter Reed and we arrived there just as he was coming out of surgery. Doctors said that with Jay's injury, it was a miracle he hadn't been killed or become a quadriplegic after what he had been through. Thank God we have the greatest military in the world and these young men and women are in such great shape because that is what saved Jay's life. I spent much of my time wandering around the hospital talking to the other patients, family members and nurses to get a better feel for how others were getting along. I also met many family members on the bus ride every day traveling back and forth between the hotel and Walter Reed.

Once employees, especially the nurses, found out I was from Illinois all anyone wanted to talk about was Barack Obama. It happened wherever I went so I wasn't surprised especially with the election less than three months away.

It did not take long, however, to learn of the debilitating injuries experienced by so many soldiers who served in Iraq and Afghanistan. I wondered if our government was doing all that was needed to support the soldiers and veterans who shouldered the burden of these two wars. Jay and I had many discussions about Afghanistan and Iraq, how they were different, and how these wars should be fought.

What you learn from the families of ordinary soldiers and what you hear officially from the generals is often a world apart. Americans were shocked by some of the sensational stories involving false information at high levels of the Pentagon, such as cover up of the "friendly fire" incident that killed former NFL player Pat Tillman or the sensational and misleading stories about Private Jessica Lynch. I met a woman at Walter Reed hospital whose son told her that ambush deaths in his unit were never reported as such. Her son was serving in the infantry in Iraq when the Hummer he was in with two others on a night mission encountered an Improvised Explosive Devise (IED) and all three were blown out of the vehicle. The vehicle was blown to smithereens and the tanker carrying 4,000 gallons of fuel was also hit. Luckily, the Hummer was in front of the fire ball and the men survived. The young soldier survived, though he was bleeding internally and had a brain trauma. They operated on him to stop the bleeding while still in Iraq. Then they flew him to Landstuhl before being shipped to Walter Reed. Two of the other injured soldiers from his unit were still in Germany.

Also at Walter Reed I met a middle aged African American man from Tennessee who was visiting his wife who had cancer and not expected to make it. She had been in the Army for sixteen years and on her third tour of duty in Iraq. She kept telling her superiors she was sick. They didn't believe her and thought she was just trying to get out of Iraq. Finally, she was assigned to escort another sick soldier home. When they got to Kuwait, this man's wife collapsed and they had to get her to Germany where she was hospitalized. The soldier's kidneys had begun to fail. They discovered she had cancer when she arrived at Walter Reed and now this man realized he was about to lose his wife because her superiors refused to believe she was sick. I have to believe there's another side to this story but war is tragic enough without such avoidable deaths.

Veteran Affairs: Shinseki and Filner

Fortunately, I had the opportunity to work with two individuals who were ready to make a difference for American veterans, whether they served in Vietnam, Korea, World War II or our most recent conflicts in Iraq and Afghanistan. They were General Eric Shinseki, Secretary of Veterans Affairs and Bob Filner, (D-CA) Chairman of the House Committee on Veterans Affairs. They couldn't have been more different in backgrounds, but they came together in ways that significantly improved the way we support our veterans. General Shinseki was a Vietnam combat veteran who lost part of his foot as a forward artillery observer when he stepped on a land mine while serving as Commander of Troop A, Third Squadron, Fifth Cavalry Regiment. Shinseki is somewhat small in stature and seemed to me surprisingly soft spoken for a general, but he was widely respected by the troops he commanded and he won over many of the veterans groups that had been frustrated for years with the Veterans Administration's previous slow response to the influx of wounded veterans. Like President Obama, he grew up in Hawaii, where his grandparents had migrated from Hiroshima in 1901. Shinseki served as Army Chief of Staff from 1999 through 2003 when he clashed with then Defense Secretary Rumsfeld over the number of troops that would be needed to successfully secure Iraq if the Bush administration carried out its plans for an invasion. Rumsfeld and his deputy Paul Wolfowitz had been trying to sell the idea that the invasion of Iraq could be done with a limited number of troops in a short campaign. Shinseki, who knew better, was asked what he thought when he was testifying before the House Armed Services Committee and said "something in the order of several hundred thousand soldiers." Rumsfeld publicly lambasted Shinseki who retired soon thereafter, but evidence showed Shinseki's prediction was correct as there were insufficient troops to maintain security when sectarian militias made Iraq an uncontrollable nightmare for its population in 2004–2005. On November 15, 2006, in testimony before Congress, CENTCOM Commander Gen. John Abizaid said that General Shinseki had been correct that more troops were needed.

Shinseki felt that a debt had never been acknowledged to Vietnam veterans and as Secretary of Veterans Affairs he wrote in the Wall Street Journal: "To Veterans of Vietnam, welcome home. That generation remembers returning from war to a country so divided and distracted by internal politics that it had little interest in what they had been doing for the nation. The slight was palpable and the memory of it has lasted decades. Hence, 'Welcome Home!' became their greeting for one another and for no one else, because it was the greeting they never received."

Veteran's Affairs Committee Chairman Bob Filner who had opposed the Vietnam War and voted against authorization for the Iraq war was among those in Congress sponsoring resolutions to establish a Welcome Home Vietnam Veteran's Day to correct this injustice to the servicemen who fought in that unpopular war. Filner was also a strong and effective ally in our efforts to make sure that the Veteran's Administration would be better equipped to support our returning veterans from Iraq and Afghanistan. Filner's activism went back to his days as an eighteen year-old freshman college student at Cornell University who became a "Freedom Rider," taking a Greyhound bus to Mississippi in 1961 as a part of the nascent civil rights movement. Filner was arrested with his co-riders and went to jail for two months refusing to post bond to protest segregation in the South.

The young Filner's conviction for "disturbing the peace and inciting a riot" was eventually overturned by a historic Supreme Court decision that overturned laws enforcing racial separation. There were two former Freedom Riders in the House of Representatives. The other was my mentor, the eminent civil rights leader Congressman John Lewis, (D-GA) a close associate of Dr. Martin Luther King who endured numerous beatings and arrests fighting injustice. Lewis led 525 peaceful marchers across the Pettus Bridge in Selma, Alabama in 1965. State troopers attacked the marchers in a violent incident that later became known as "Bloody Sunday" that became a legendary turning point in the civil rights movement.

Of course conservatives were never very comfortable with Filner because of his past, but he used humor to defuse their hostility especially that of Republican Congressman Steve Buyer (D-IN). He was the ranking member of the House Committee on Veterans' Affairs who was often the lone holdout vote while putting together a team effort to pass major veterans legislation. Sometimes he never came around and eventually voted no for the final bill just because of his disdain for Filner. Different members were assigned to put together specific parts of the overall legislation and I was fortunate that Chairman Filner put so much confidence in my ability to lead many of those efforts.

I had learned a great deal about issues that wounded veterans faced in conversations with families and staff at Walter Reed following Jay's recovery and the good news was that the quality of medical care at our best facilities was saving lives and limbs that would have been impossible a decade ago. A number of successful surgeries and Jay's training in Special Forces helped get him back on his feet again. Although he lives with some pain, he was able to continue serving in the armed forces. While he was rehabilitating he worked in Washington, DC, for Special Operations Communication (SOCOM) and attended Georgetown University. He is now married and as of May 9, 2012, he and his wife, Ellen, have a beautiful daughter Julia. Jay is currently a Major in the Army serving at Eglin Air Force Base in Florida.

Trip To the Middle East

To learn first hand about medical care on the battlefield members of the Veteran's Affairs Subcommittee on Health took a trip during one of our district work periods in 2009 to visit US bases in the Middle East. It was necessary to get a first hand view of the war that many Americans knew so little about despite the mounting sacrifices of our military men and women.

I am just as conflicted now as I was then about being somewhere that has cost so many American lives, has cost billions of dollars and still doesn't have a clear strategy of success.

But our mission was health care and making sure every returning soldier as well as current veterans have a streamlined system something that most people felt was far off from happening. Other than myself, Congressmen Mike Michaud (D-ME), Tom Perriello (D-VA), Glenn Nye (D-VA) and Phil Roe (R-TN) were accompanied with experts from the Army as well as the Navy. After a stop in Kuwait we flew to the large US base in Bagram, Afghanistan. We were briefed by different units about the varying quality of on-site medical care across the theater of battle. We found that it varied widely from the very rudimentary (bandages and antiseptics) to more sophisticated on-site medical care. The challenge was often how quickly injured soldiers could be transported to the base hospital in Bagram and on to Landstuhl, Germany.

I have to admit that sleeping in the Bagram barracks was a bit eerie. I slept in my clothes as well as socks and shoes, in bunk beds covered by a blanket in a large upstairs space. During the night there were regular bursts of nearby gunfire. At first I could not tell if the noise was from a practice range or an imminent enemy attack until we received a knock on our door to inform us. It is unfortunate that most of what is going on with these decade long wars are so far away in the minds of most Americans. I wonder if things would have been any different if more members of Congress had felt the pain of war in their own families like myself and so many other families all over America. I guess out of sight, out of mind.

The base commander arranged it so that we ate in the large mess hall with troops from our home state. The food was healthy and labeled explaining exactly the number of calories, carbohydrates and other nutritional values. Soldiers were friendly and dedicated to their mission, but it was clear that they were living and operating in an extremely stressful environment. Each soldier sat down to eat with their rifle by his or her side a reminder of the unpredictable environment where stretches of boredom often were punctuated by sudden violent battles.

Our subcommittee members then continued to follow the path of wounded soldiers by flying to the hospital in Landstuhl, Germany. It was an emotional event for both the medical staff there and myself because they had had just tended to Jay seven months before and said they almost never get a chance to meet the relatives of those whose lives they helped save. I gave a heart felt speech to thank them all for saving Jay's life and to let them know how he was doing. The staff posed for pictures with me in front of the hospital. We spent time being briefed on the operations of the hospital which were modern with a highly experienced staff. The records of wounded soldiers like Jay were computerized and complete, though this was not the case for previous generations of soldiers. It is the goal of the Veterans' Administration (VA) to eventually have computerized records for all veterans. What a treat that will be for our veterans who have so much trouble with paperwork being lost in the system only to find they have no benefits. I believe I was one of if not the only member with a full time case worker that did nothing but work on veterans issues. It was so rewarding to be able to see the smile on their face when they knew there was someone from my office who cared enough to stay by their side to get what was rightfully theirs when they had run into road blocks and dead ends for years.

My Work With Soldiers and Veterans

While working in Washington, DC, my staff kept in close contact with constituents that ended up in Walter Reed Hospital due to Iraq or Afghanistan injuries. Within a few days we were able to arrange for me to visit the injured soldiers from my district to show my support for the family. The hardest phone calls to make were to the loved ones who lost their lives in the line of duty or worse yet—to suicide.

Working closely with Chairman Filner I managed several veteran's bills in the House that were part of the comprehensive Veteran Administration legislation that significantly increased services and resources available to veterans. Managing a bill means you are in charge of the bill on the floor of the House. I know many of you reading this book who have watched C-Span are saying to yourself there is never anyone on the House floor. This is a very good time to explain why it seems empty. During debate of legislation there are two managers of the bills, one from each party and they are normally the committee chairman and the ranking member. As the bill is read and debated for the Congressional Record, members of Congress who have amendments to the bill approach the microphone to talk about their part of the bill. Sometimes members come and go to talk about the bill without having an amendment. That is why it looks empty. The remaining members are in committee hearings, meetings, on the phone or in their office watching debate on their own monitor like many of you do at home. The Representatives typically don't come to the House chamber until they get notification that it is time to vote either from a pager they wear or from the wall clock in their office. The clock then starts and the first vote is typically fifteen minutes long. Once in the chamber subsequent votes are five minutes long.

When I managed my first set of bills, the Speaker and Majority Leader's staffs were on hand to help, but I made sure I was well prepared for any issues that might arise from Republicans on the floor. I came from twelve years of legislative experience but anything was possible when it came to the other side trying to take those of us who were new, off our game.

One of the bills I sponsored that became law was a bill to eliminate co-payments that veterans pay when catastrophically injured. It made no sense to me that hard pressed veterans, many of them out of work—should have a co-pay to see a doctor. The co-payments were an extra burden that catastrophically disabled veterans and their families not only didn't need but couldn't afford. On another front, as a woman and a mother, I understood that the quality of long term care would depend on wives, mothers or other relatives and they were going to need training and support. I was an enthusiastic supporter and sponsor of legislation that authorized the VA to provide these resources. Many of our veterans returning from Iraq or Afghanistan with brain-damage or other severe wounds had family members who had to quit their jobs, putting financial strain on families. As voluntary caregivers they also received little or no training in delivering that care. In support of this new measure Chairman Filner noted, "We had a young lady who testified she hurt her back because she didn't know how to get her husband out of the wheelchair," Filner said. "And when you're dealing with this for twenty-four hours a day you need some rest yourself [and] to bring in people to take care of that." He added that the new law we were preparing will provide pay "to make up for loss of income; training to the caregiver; funds for respite care and some other expenses. It's not just the young man or woman who comes home [who is changed]. It's the whole family involved and we've got to help the whole family." For those veterans living in rural areas away from VA facilities, these problems were much more of a challenge.

Throughout our efforts to assemble a strong legislative package we had good access and a good working relations with VA Secretary, Shinseki. He was accessible to us as individual members when needed and we were able to go over issues that our constituents had raised with him informally at breakfast meetings. Revamping such a large, tradition-bound organization as the VA was an enormous challenge. The needs of the hundreds of thousands of new veterans from Iraq and Afghanistan were so great that there was bound to be criticism from time to time. Members of our committee found him open and responsive to our concerns and committed to improving the lives of fellow veterans. Like many of us, Secretary Shinseki was aware that a significant portion of the homeless population in American cities were veterans who had served their country. In committee hearings, I pointed out that it is nearly impossible for a homeless veteran to apply for a job if he doesn't have a phone or address to receive mail. Shinseki's commitment to end homelessness within five years of taking on the position was a worthy goal and one I hope he is held to.

The *Caregivers and Veterans Omnibus Health Services Act* (SB 1963) that passed the House and Senate in April of 2010 directs the VA to provide training and medical coverage to caregivers, to include stress counseling if needed. The *Civilian Health and Medical Program of the Department of Veterans Affairs* (CHAMPVA) would be made available to caregivers who have no health insurance options. The VA will now pay for lodging and meals to those who accompany severely injured veterans on long trips for VA health care evaluation and treatments. When a caregiver needs respite the VA will pay for temporary caregiver replacements for up to thirty days a year. Among other features of the bill:

- Expanded VA services for 1.8 million women veterans currently receiving VA care or expected to enroll in the system. The VA for the first time will cover up to seven days of newborn care for enrolled female veterans. Other initiatives will force changes to the VA health system to make it respectful of privacy and other needs of female veterans. The VA is directed to also launch a pilot program for providing patient childcare services.
- Improved health care options for rural veterans by authorizing stronger partnerships with community providers and the Department of Health and Human Services. The VA will also establish a grant program for veteran service organizations to provide transportation options to veterans in highly rural areas needing medical care.
- Expanded VA locations that provide support services to homeless veterans.
- Requires the VA to study veterans' suicides and provide counseling referrals for members of the armed forces who are not otherwise eligible for VA readjustment counseling.

Upon passage of the bill, Chairman Filner stressed that the bill would provide "access for people who don't normally have access like women. It's time to think about childcare, privacy curtains, and to think about respect." Such a change would improve the atmosphere of VA hospitals. "Older veterans will find it refreshing," he said, "to see children of women veterans, from time to time, in waiting areas of VA medical facilities. It changes the whole ambiance of the place," Filner said. "It's no longer a bunch of dying people. There's life! And so? . . . childcare not only helps the families with kids but the whole atmosphere." His words reminded me of a room in Walter Reed Hospital where I saw numerous young men moving in wheel chairs. Despite a stump of a leg which was still not fitted for a prosthetic limb, one young vet was zipping around on his wheelchair laughing with his young child who was enjoying the ride.

Our efforts and those of our counterparts in the Senate were no doubt aided by the public attention that First Lady, Michelle Obama, brought to the issue through her visits with veterans, their organizations and her public comments. Some of Obama's best speeches as president were those addressed to American servicemen and women. All of this helped create a backdrop that enabled Congress to put through a significant boost in advance funding enabling the VA to respond to the rise in wounded veterans and expansion of services without being held hostage by yearly partisan squabbles.

Legislation, however, needed to be complemented by strong constituent service and advocacy for veterans and their families in my district. We received hundreds of complaints from veterans and my office was able to help many of them because of my specialized caseworker. Payments or benefits were often very late in arriving or didn't arrive at all. This made life needlessly difficult for many veterans who were struggling financially. One constituent was owed $30,000 in accumulated benefits but had a hard time getting paid until we hectored the bureaucracy into providing the large sum that the veteran was owed. Surprisingly to me many servicemen also reported they never received medals they were were owed for years. This became another vexing issue we routinely dealt with on behalf of veterans who had displayed valor on the battle field and deserved a visible memento of their service to the country and we gave them the public ceremony they so justly deserved.

Silver Cross to Become A Veterans Mega Clinic

Probably the most important and lasting service to veterans that engaged my office was our effort to acquire the former Silver Cross Hospital Building in Joliet and transform it into a modern Veterans Administration Mega Clinic. Silver Cross was a large building and an ideal setting for a VA Hospital that would bring jobs to the area and provide a local alternative for veterans who would otherwise have to travel to Chicago. There were many steps involved in transforming the former hospital to a VA facility and my staff got to work on the logistics while I focused my efforts on winning the active support of Secretary Shinseki. It got to the point that whenever our House Committee on Veterans' Affairs met with the VA Secretary he knew my first question would be about progress on developing the Veterans Mega Clinic on the Silver Cross site. As a result, he had his staff ready with an update on developments. Chairman Filner even visited the site and was so impressed he wanted the entire hospital to be purchased because the rest of the hospital could be able to accommodate the homeless veterans in the area. The process of creating a modern VA Clinic with up-to-the minute medical technology and services takes time, but having laid the groundwork and moved the development through various phases, the project is on track for a groundbreaking. I will be quite happy to watch from the outside as the finishing touches are put on a project I know will help so many deserving men and women. With the end of the Iraq war and the the Afghanistan war near its end, this facility will be needed more than ever. It is my hope that whoever serves that area in the future has the passion as I did to make it even bigger and better as time and need goes on. It has been such an honor to serve the veterans of not only my district but the entire country even if it was just a short two years. I will never forget the honor I was given by the citizens to serve. I also want to thank James Canup, a Vietnam veteran from Braidwood who's passion and commitment was relentless in moving this project forward; and who worked diligently to bring so many others along with him.

Abraham Lincoln National Cemetery

President Obama had made stirring speeches to active duty soldiers and veterans at institutions such as West Point and the US base Yongsan Garrison in South Korea on special holidays so I was delighted when President Obama decided to give a Memorial Day speech in my district at the relatively new Abraham Lincoln National Cemetery which is the largest veteran burial site in the US and when fully completed will have 400,000 available graves. It is built on land previously owned by the Joliet Arsenal and was named after our sixteenth president, who established the first national cemeteries during the Civil War. Among those buried there is a Medal of Honor recipient from the Civil War Battle of Vicksburg and the late Congressman George Sangmeister a well respected Korean War veteran who was key in establishing the cemetery. He served in Congress from 1988 to 1994.

On Memorial Day there were more than 10,000 people at the Abraham Lincoln National Cemetery waiting to hear President Obama speak, including Senator Durbin, myself and State Treasurer Alexi Gianoulias, (an Obama friend and basketball teammate) who was a candidate for Obama's US Senate seat. It was a very warm day and not a cloud in the sky. People had gathered and were waiting for the President to arrive. Many of my family members were in the audience including my parents who were visiting from Florida. As everyone watched Marine One come into view the crowd started to cheer and clouds began to gather. Once the President's entourage landed the sound of thunder echoed and rain began to fall. The President was about to take the stage and the drizzle turned into a downpour along with dangerous lightening. Secret Service forbid the President to take to the stage given the lighting and thunder nearby. Obama was equally adamant that he needed to at least inform the large crowd—many of them veterans and their families—that he still hoped to give his speech when the rain subsided. It became a heated standoff between President Obama and the Secret Service. My granddaughter, Ellie, who was in the front row with her parents was very wet by this time as well as frightened by all of the thunder and began crying and calling out for me. As I got up to lift Ellie over the barrier the Secret Service agents did their job by stopping me from getting her. When President Obama saw that it was Ellie he brushed aside the Secret Service and told State Treasurer Gianoulias to go out in the torrential rain to get her and bring Ellie back to be with us under the tent. He did so immediately and the President made her feel much better. Meanwhile, Senator Durbin advised the Secret Service that they were not going to stop the President from speaking to the crowd of more than 10,000 people who were still waiting there to hear him speak. At that point the Secret Service reluctantly handed Obama a very large umbrella (probably not a smart move since it was lightning) so he could take the stage amidst the downpour to welcome the crowd and explain that he still hoped to give his speech but if the rain had not stopped in thirty minutes people should return to the buses that brought them to the site from the parking lot. Some of the crowd returned to the buses but most stayed in place huddled under their umbrellas that had been turned inside out by the wind while the rain continued unabated. Soon it became apparent that the rain was not going to stop and Obama would not be giving his speech to the crowd. He did stop at different buses where people were waiting. President Obama offered a few of the points he had intended to make in the keynote speech while the majority of the crowd was stuck in the rain waiting for the buses to return for them. From what I've observed, Obama deeply felt the burden of the losses in Iraq and Afghanistan and though he opposed the war in Iraq he felt strongly that every effort needed to be made to show gratitude for the soldiers, sailors and airmen who sacrificed so much.

Constituent Service/Committee Work

I met regularly with my Veterans Advisory Committee who I considered my experts on the issues. I often held town hall meetings for my veterans, accompanied by Illinois Veteran Affairs Director, Tammy Duckworth, so that they could speak up about problems they were encountering. There were many issues but for most veterans the overriding concern was not getting the benefits they were due. When it came to the younger veterans the issue was finding work in an economy where so many others were unemployed. To their credit the hard pressed construction industry—the contractors associations and unions—put together a program called "From Helmets to Hardhats" to give veterans a chance to use their service as a credit in building a profile in the industry. Veterans were able to train and were given priority for job openings. The program also connected them with other veterans who had made the transition from battlefield to peacetime construction. In a Wall Street Journal column Secretary Shinseki made the case that veterans make "exceptional employees" and companies would benefit by hiring them: "Veterans bring a positive mission-first no-fail no-quit attitude to any organization they join. They have been an extraordinary force for good—whether capturing Saddam Hussein, delivering justice to Osama bin Laden, or working with local leaders and training the military forces of both Afghanistan and Iraq to assume responsibility for their own defense. They are value-added to any organization." Despite the disabilities that many of these veterans have suffered I couldn't agree more with Shinseki's description of what veterans can bring to the companies that hire them.

11

The (Polarized) Congress That Couldn't

Great minds discuss ideas, average minds discuss events,
small minds discuss people
—Eleanor Roosevelt

Obama's First Bill–Lilly Ledbetter Act

By the second year of the Obama presidency, polarization in Congress had led to increased suspicion and hostility between the two parties. While Democrats often were at odds with themselves on the issues of taxes, the budget and the energy bill, Republican members of the House of Representatives seemed to march lockstep in opposition to any legislation proposed by the President and his allies in Congress.

The very first bill that passed under the new Obama administration was the *Lilly Ledbetter Fair Pay Act* of 2009, signed by the President on January 29, 2009. This Act amends the *Civil Rights Act of 1964* stating that the 180 day statute of limitations for filing an equal-pay lawsuit regarding pay discrimination resets with each new discriminatory paycheck.

Unfortunately this bill which strengthened laws guaranteeing equal pay for equal work, did not receive a single Republican vote. As someone who believed that women should uphold the values of gender equality regardless of party I was quite frankly disappointed in the Republican women who fell meekly into line with House Republican leaders John Boehner (D-OH) and Eric Cantor (D-VA). When I was in the Illinois state Senate, I regularly confronted the Republican women on how could they claim they supported women's rights when they constantly followed their male leaders like James "Pate" Phillips who was a self proclaimed male chauvinist. The women in his caucus never found a way to publicly speak up against him. They seem to have come a long way now that they have a female Minority Leader in the Senate—Chris Rodogno.

Lilly Ledbetter, for whom the bill had been named, was a production supervisor at a Goodyear tire plant who filed a lawsuit under the 1964 *Civil Rights Act* alleging pay discrimination. The lower court's award to her was overturned by a five to four Supreme Court decision arguing that she had not filed her lawsuit within 180 days of the company's decision to pay her less than male counterparts as required. A minority opinion written by Supreme Court Justice Ruth Ginsberg argued that the law could have been applied within 180 days of any discriminatory paycheck Ms. Ledbetter received. Debra Ness, president of the National Partnership for Women & Families condemned the majority decision saying its message was, "If employers can keep the discrimination hidden for a period of time, they can continue to discriminate without being held accountable." Women's organizations and their allies in Congress moved to clarify the law in light of the Supreme Court decision once Obama took office. Lilly Ledbetter's long struggle resulted in a bill bearing her name and she was on hand when President Obama signed the legislation. The unanimity of the Republicans in opposing an issue of basic fairness more than forty years after the historic civil rights legislation of 1964 was an early warning sign that did not bode well for the possibilities of cooperation and comity in Congress.

American Recovery and Reinvestment Act

Republicans voted overwhelmingly against any legislation they had previously been in support of if the President now supported it. The *American Recovery and Reinvestment Act* (ARRA) was signed by the President on February 17, 2009. It contained the largest middle class tax cut in history (thirty seven percent of the bill or $288 billion) but did not get a single Republican vote. The primary objective for ARRA was to save and create jobs almost immediately. The secondary objectives were to provide temporary relief programs for those most impacted by the recession and invest in infrastructure, education, health, and 'green' energy. The approximate cost of the economic stimulus package was estimated to be $787 billion at the time of passage, later revised to $831 billion. The Act included direct spending on infrastructure, education, health, and energy, federal tax incentives, and expansion of unemployment benefits.

According to *The Blue Green Alliance and Economic Policy Institute*, ARRA was a response to the great financial crash of 2008 that devastated the US economy, destroyed millions of jobs, created millions more long-term unemployed and forced a tax-payer bailout unparalleled in American history. The ARRA's enactment represented a dramatic attempt to resuscitate a US economy in free-fall.

Two years later, the Recovery Act's public investments have not only saved and created millions of jobs, but have also represented an unprecedented down payment on the nation's emerging green economy. As outlined in this report, *Rebuilding Green: The American Recovery and Reinvestment Act and the Green Economy,* the success of that down payment makes a strong case for additional public investment in the green economy as a centerpiece of a national strategy to solve the continuing unemployment crisis."

American Clean Energy and Security Act

The Democrats also had a problem messaging the *American Clean Energy and Security Act* (ACES) sponsored by Representative Henry Waxman (D-CA). Once the bill passed the House, it stalled in the Senate. The bill which was referred to as the climate change bill, or cap and trade bill, cap and tax was intended to create clean energy jobs, achieve energy independence, reduce global warming pollution and transition to a clean energy economy. It also set economic incentives for industries to reduce emissions and subsidized the development of renewable energy (wind, solar, geothermal). It protected consumers from energy price increases. By gradually lowering the total national emissions as technology improved and alternative energy sources became cheaper, the bill was expected to cut emissions by eighty percent as of 2050. A Congressional Budget Office (CBO) analysis found that it was revenue neutral. No one believed the CBO analysis and Democrats lost the message war. We never did get credit on just how necessary it was to have an energy bill move to the Senate to keep the discussion moving on having an energy policy for the country.

I was a cosponsor of language that became part of the bill including a "Clean Energy Investment Fund" to provide market security and access to investors in new, domestic clean energy products and technologies. This is important because 2700 jobs are created for every $100 million in venture capital investment. I also cosponsored a $30 billion Manufacturing Revolving Fund where states receive grants to establish loan funds to assist firms in retooling, expanding or establishing clean energy operations and energy efficiency. These loans provide liquidity and improve the competitive position of our domestic industry. As I conducted meetings around the district about the energy bill, the message I received loud and clear was we needed to do something to stop our jobs from leaving the country and help manufacturing here in America become more competitive and energy efficient. I went back to DC, and fought to add language into the energy bill that would accomplish exactly what people said they wanted. That is where the $30 billion Manufacturing Revolving Fund came from. What amazed me was when I went back to those groups, excited about what I was able to get into the bill for them those same people were still vehemently opposed to the bill for no other reason than to say they didn't believe I could get it done and they didn't like other parts of the bill. That was the case not only in this bill but in most everything we did.

It was unfortunate that the administration felt the need to rush the energy bill through the House in time for the International Conference in Copenhagen because there were many good features in the bill, though most Republicans and a number of Blue Dog Democrats thought it was too tough on the polluting industries. I really do believe if the leadership was not in such a hurry we may have had a chance to get meaningful legislation passed.

While many environmental groups, such as the Environment Defense Fund supported the legislation, Greenpeace and Friends of the Earth opposed it because they felt it became too weak following some added amendments. When the same kinds of groups support and oppose legislation all at the same time, it is no wonder the Democrats continuously lose the message war. Then you had Shell Oil, Duke Energy and Exelon who supported the bill which didn't help with some environmentalists and progressive Democrats like Dennis Kucinich (D-OH) and Pete Stark (D-CA) who opposed the bill.

I had my own problems with the legislation but overall I knew we needed an energy policy and the only way to keep the conversation going was to move it over to the Senate. Isn't that what politics is supposed to be about: the art of negotiation? I was used to being a team player, to not judge the process but the final product. What I was not used to were these thousand page bills that contained everything but the kitchen sink. In Illinois all bills were germane to a single subject and if it didn't pertain to that one subject it went into a new bill. If I could change one thing about Washington (even though there were plenty of things to change), I would make all bills single subject, not these packages of bills that give everyone something to vote for or against and bills that give the public reason to be skeptical of this body of government.

President Obama had critics who thought he missed a good opportunity to use the massive BP oil spill in the Gulf of Mexico (the worst environmental disaster in US history) to move the energy bill forward in the Senate. Ironically, however, the BP oil spill actually helped undo the core of a possible bipartisan agreement worked out with Senator John Kerry, Joe Lieberman and Lindsey Graham that might have enabled the Senate to reach the needed sixty votes for cloture (to end debate and vote). The expansion of offshore drilling was a key element, however, and after the BP oil spill, expansion of off shore drilling was no longer a possibility. Once the deal fell apart, some key utility companies which had held their fire while a deal was being considered, came out strongly in opposition working with a coalition of Republicans and coal state Democrats to block the bill in the Senate.

The *American Clean Energy Security Act* (ACES) bill, would have been an important step forward toward clean, affordable energy. Passage of the bill would have created far more jobs than would be lost short term. In Illinois alone, two studies showed that it would have created 70,000 jobs, most of them in manufacturing. The tax credits for wind energy would have been a further boon for wind farms like those being built by the Horizon Wind Energy company in my district that would provide energy to operate 180,000 homes when all phases of the program have been completed. Studies showed that Illinois would have been number two on a list of states that could create jobs in solar industries and third on the list in producing wind energy. I do not think most people of Illinois realize that there is already a renewable standards law in place that spells out by the year 2025, twenty-five percent of all electricity must come from renewable sources.

The defeat of the energy bill has emboldened those who talk about abolishing or defunding the EPA and that is a serious problem. Frank O'Donnell, President of Clean Air Watch, acknowledged that environmentalists need to do a better job reaching ordinary Americans and explaining the benefits of legislation like ACES. For his part, O'Donnell said his community didn't focus enough on what was happening away from the White House and Capitol Hill. "Environmental groups failed to build a genuine outside-the-beltway support for it," O'Donnell said. "Too much of it was inside-the-beltway lobbying that didn't translate. I don't know that the public outside the beltway was sufficiently engaged."

During the summer of 2012, most of the country encountered more than one hundred degree heat and in the Midwest the least amount of rain on record. The debate continues about global warming. If you get people in the right setting that have some familiarity with the issues, it's a lot easier to get out the message that safe renewable energy creates jobs, will improve the environment and reduce our dependence on foreign oil. There is much work to be done and even the President of the United States found out that you can't sit inside the beltway, continue to believe your own press releases and think that everything is going to be all right. This is a continuing problem that is not going away and if we care about the earth our grandchildren and great-grandchildren are going to live on something needs to be done. Hopefully it is not too late.

I recall a Home Depot tour I had about energy efficient products in January of 2010. When I arrived there were about twenty employees to greet me in front of the store, including employees from several surrounding stores. They presented me with my own autographed orange apron with my name on it. It was clear that those who worked with energy efficient products were not only receptive to the goals of the legislation we were working on, they were exactly the kind of well informed individuals who could explain to others the benefits of public policies that promote conservation and clean energy.

I was also running for re-election at the time and I approached their federal Political Action Committee (PAC) who had previously supported me for a contribution. Their PAC Board who must not be made up of energy conscious people like the employees I had just been with decided to support my Republican opponent. I felt sorry for their lobbyist who had to deliver the bad news because this board should have been happy with me. Yes, the Home Depot Federal PAC was opposed to the energy bill. I call that cutting your nose off to spite your face.

News? Truth?

For some reason, people decided they would rather believe the lies they heard from the TV and radio programs, pundits and other extremists who had no intention of doing anything but poison the minds of as many people as possible against this administration. At the end of a long day, I would go to my apartment, warm up a bowl of soup for dinner and turn on the news. Most of the time I would shake my head because that wasn't the Capitol I spent the day at. It's a shame how news is reported. Where are people supposed to get the truth?

Jobs, Jobs, Jobs and the Hire Act

Throughout the 111th Congress, I worked with small businesses to explore what they needed to expand and create jobs by holding business round tables to hear directly from small business leaders about what they needed most. Typically, I heard about the need to bring confidence back as well as the uncertainty in the economy which made business owners reluctant to invest. More specifically, they said: "The banks aren't loaning."

The banks blamed regulators and vice-a versa. We questioned them extensively and to some degree both sides were right. The policies of the regulators (designed to prevent the kind of meltdown the country experienced in 2008) were intimidating the banks and the banks were clearly holding back on loans needed to restore business confidence and expand their operations. Breaking through this vicious circle became our urgent quest. One answer was to expand the Small Business Administration's (SBA) ability to guarantee private loans. I arranged for Karen Mills, Director, of the SBA to visit my district and speak with businesses about how to make the best use of the agency to pursue business opportunities. I also arranged entrepreneurial "boot camps" for job hunters in my district. There were opportunities for people who needed to build their job skills to receive mentoring and opportunities to obtain business loans to start new businesses

Working with small businesses I was one of the authors of the *Hiring Incentives to Restore Employment Act*—or the Hire Act, which gave specific tax break to hire unemployed workers including a payroll tax exemption of the employer's share of payroll taxes on any wages paid after March 18, 2010. Employers also received a tax credit of $1000 per worker hired. The goal was to put Americans back to work as soon as possible. Business owners that hired qualifying workers sooner rather than later would get the most out of the tax credits because the tax credits diminished over time. The bill also included an amendment I sponsored to allow employers to depreciate the purchase of equipment they bought up to $250,000 on their taxes within the first year instead of over time in order to encourage immediate investments into their companies especially manufacturing. The bill also had provisions for putting people to work by reforming municipal bonds. Build America Bonds were designed to allow the money to be spent on construction &

repair of public projects like schools, highway and transit programs, as well as green and clean energy conservation projects like wind turbines and solar energy devices. Some of this money came from moving $20 billion into the highway trust fund. I was honored to be with President Obama when he signed the *Hire Act* which originally passed the House in 2009, but was scaled down considerably by the time it passed through the Senate and the differences worked out in Conference Committee.

Those who understood my efforts in Washington were supportive. For instance, I had worked closely with Jerry Roper, Chairman of the Chicagoland Chamber of Commerce and his Executive Director Jim Ferrell. Following a speech I gave there in June of 2009, Ferrell took the microphone and said "The Congresswoman is being too polite. Let me tell you what she has done in the first ninety days of being in Congress" and talked about projects and legislation that we worked on together. He finished adding "Debbie Halvorson knows what she's doing and it's like all she had to do was flip on a switch for $137 million in projects she brought back in just ninety days. Watch this woman. She's going places." I'm sure I was blushing at the time. Yet, over the next year, following the effects of a bad economy the local controversies over the energy bill, the rise of the Tea Party and a relentless pounding of the Obama administration by Fox News, talk radio and conservative blogs, I was being portrayed by my opponents as unfriendly to business and a pawn of Nancy Pelosi. I spoke in Bloomington, the southern part of my district, and the local head of the Chamber of Commerce publicly went on about how I was "ruining the country" by supporting an energy policy even though it never cleared the Senate and which I doubted he could describe in any detail. I and others who spoke at that meeting thought the man had embarrassed himself with his harangue, but it was the kind of the thing I was regularly encountering from Tea Party types in town hall meetings and other forums.

Words Like Compromise and Negotiation Not Allowed

I expected that after the Tea Party's flush of victory, voters would begin to have buyer's remorse. They did and it happened rather quickly the following year when Tea Party stalwarts repeatedly threatened to shut government down if their demands were not met on radical deficit reduction.

In the first chapter of this book I mentioned the President's call asking me what I thought about a compromise with the Republican on renewing the Bush tax cuts in return for Republican support for a number important bills that had been held hostage. Like the President, I would have strongly preferred extending the tax cuts only to those ninety-eight percent of Americans making less than $250,000 a year, but ultimately we extended them all so we could get other things done. That was a worthwhile compromise which led to the most productive lame duck session of Congress in memory. "Don't Ask Don't Tell legislation which discriminated against gays in the military was quickly passed. The Senate START Treaty, which had been bottled up despite bipartisan support was also allowed to pass followed by the long delayed bill to compensate the heroic 9/11 first responders who suffered terribly from health problems they acquired at the ruins of the World Trade Center.

Finally there was the passage of the *Healthy, Hunger Free Kids Act and the Food Safety and Modernization Act* passed on January 4 of 2011 which added to a remarkably productive, turbulent and controversial Congressional session that I had a chance to participate in fully from beginning to end.

12

Jesse Jackson Jr.—A Talented and Troubled Man

The biggest person with the biggest ideas can be shot down by the smallest person with the smallest mind. Think big anyway
—Mother Teresa

I have to admit, this has been the most difficult chapter to write. It has been challenging on so many counts. The biggest challenge was finding a place to end the seemingly endless saga.

With an ethics investigation and general election still looming I am sure someone else will write the rest of the on going saga of Jesse Jackson, Jr. At this point in the story he has returned home to Washington, DC after over a month at Mayo Clinic in Minnesota having been treated for Bipolar condition and the congressman listed his $2.5 million Washington, DC home for sale. There had been discussion as to whether he would return to work or even campaign before the November election: he will not. Congress has adjourned until after the election.

After Jackson's spokesman released a statement that the congressman would be taking a medical leave of absence, criticism kept building and more people were asking for information about the congressman's where abouts. His staff finally realized for the first time, Jesse Jackson, Jr., could not continue acting like royalty as he was accustomed to. In the past, when things got tough for Jesse he found it easier to run away from his problems and that wasn't working anymore. Jesse had already been on his medical leave for ten days before anyone noticed his absence. If you remember just the year before Representative Anthony Weiner (D-NY) was run out of office in just a couple of weeks for taking lewd pictures of himself and sending them out on his twitter account. Not only had the press been asking that the congressman or his staff give out more information about what was really wrong and when would he return, but the questioning was now coming from his colleagues, Luis Gutierrez (D-IL) and Dick Durbin (D-IL) to Steny Hoyer (D-MD) just to name a few.

Then came the news that the Illinois congressman's condition was "more serious" than initially believed. It was recently revealed that the Democrat went on medical leave June 10 and was being treated for exhaustion. "Recently we have been made aware that he has grappled with certain physical and emotional ailments privately for a long period of time," a statement put out by the congressman's staff said. "At present he is undergoing further evaluation and treatment at an inpatient facility." Watkins said in a statement Jackson will need "extended in-patient treatment as well as continuing medical treatment."

Finally on Thursday, July 12, 2012, as rumors kept surfacing such as suicide attempts, alcoholism and cancer his staff issued another statement, this time thinking they would clear the air for good. The revelation that he was being treated for a "mood disorder" at an impatient center probably somewhere in Arizona still did nothing to tamp down the wide spread speculation of what was really going on. Doctors say a mood disorder is an overarching category that includes conditions such as clinical depression and bipolar disorder that involves feeling extreme highs and lows. It is the brain's inability to properly regulate mood, which leads to suicidal thoughts etc. This makes the decision making process next to impossible.

In fact, since reporters could not seem to find anyone close to Jackson in Washington, Politico and other DC news sources sent reporters to the area trying to find anyone who may be close to the congressman to get any kind of "inside scoop" regarding how the constituents would put up with their representative behaving in such a way.

Jackson has had problems for quite some time and I didn't run against him to be mean or vindictive. If Jesse had been doing his job there would have been no reason to challenge him in the Democratic primary. I ran against him because I knew that I could do better and this district was going to need someone who would be around to represent the people.

The representative's mother even acknowledged that his depression worsened when he did not become Mayor of Chicago and wasn't handed the job to replace Obama as US Senator. Many who have worked with Representative Jackson say this is the person who really does believe he is royalty and has a strong sense of entitlement rather than a work ethic. In my opinion he is clearly bored being the Congressman of Illinois-2. He doesn't really want to do the job, he wants to *be someone* on the national stage.

Chicago area columnists like Phil Kadner and Mary Mitchell protected him for many years. Most columnists and pundits are saying he has no future beyond where he is today. When Mary Mitchell, a popular African American Columnist for the

Chicago Sun-Times writes an unflattering column about Jesse, we know there are problems. This from from Mary Mitchell's column of July 12, 2012:

> It pays to be royalty. What other elected official would get the consideration that US Rep. Jesse Jackson Jr. is getting? It is an extreme dereliction of his duties. Yet there is a downside for Jackson. The protracted secrecy is fueling a lot of speculation about the congressman's future. On Wednesday, his office released yet another brief statement, this one revealing that he is being treated for an unspecified mood disorder. But it offered no details and raised even more questions. "But the statement began by quoting federal laws protecting a patient's privacy. "The name of the attending physician and treatment center will not be disclosed in order to protect his continuing privacy," the statement read. But those laws should not be used to give an elected official cover to withhold information. Jackson's duty is to be transparent and keep his constituents informed about anything that could affect the job they elected him to do. But he is still facing a House Ethics Committee probe into whether he had knowledge that Raghuveer Nayak, a fund-raiser and friend, allegedly acted as an emissary in a scheme to buy an appointment to President Barack Obama's US Senate seat. Although the congressman has not been charged with any wrongdoing, his reputation took a hit and he's kept a low profile ever since. For someone who is used to basking in the light, not hiding from it, Jackson must have chafed at other revelations about his personal life. And while voters forgive and forget, the feds do not. But the price of royalty is duty. Jackson's constituents shouldn't have to wade through a storm of speculation to get to the truth about what has sidelined their champion.

Jesse could have been somebody, but his personal agenda got in the way at every turn he made. Much of my state Senate district was within his congressional district and we tolerated each other. The bad blood really was between Emil Jones and Jackson but since I was on Emil's "team" Jesse decided I was the enemy also. It was a shame he played those games but it was to his detriment. Everything Jesse did had to have a winner and a loser and he spent more time pitting people against one another instead of getting people to work together. That is why he became involved in almost every local election. Jesse wanted to be a king maker.

Jesse and I worked together when we could. One of those times occurred when I was Chair of the newly formed caucus of Southland legislators. The Southland Caucus was made up of Senate and House members, Democrats and Republicans. Our main mission was to stand together for the betterment of the South Suburbs of Chicago. We worked best on transportation issues because roads, bridges and airports were not partisan issues. We had worked hard to make sure there was money for passenger rail service. The Chairman of our passenger rail service, Metra, Jeff Ladd had made a very unfortunate remark about the Southland area and decided the money set aside for us would be better used somewhere else. Representative Jackson and myself went directly to Mr. Ladd's office to rectify the issue immediately.

South Suburban Airport

Our biggest disagreement involved the proposed South Suburban Airport. The airport never was in any part of Illinois-2 and until the year 2002 it was in Larry Walsh's state Senate district. In 2002 after the new map was drawn I was moved further south and Larry Walsh was moved west, the South Suburban Airport footprint became part of my district. That is when I took on the issue.

Between 2002 and 2005 I worked with the local mayors putting together a development district as well as a governance plan for the proposed airport. Both were passed by the state Senate but not the House.

Jessie and I actually agreed on most policy issues and were both close to President Obama who, after becoming a US Senator, sought to mediate the third airport issue. Jackson was very combative against anyone who opposed his particular plan, firing off press releases against me and withdrawing his support from members of the delegation who disagreed with his plan. When Democrat Glenn Poshard was running for Governor, Congressman Jackson backed Republican George Ryan because of his support for the airport, but I was not one to roll over when important issues involving my district were at stake.

I thought I had seen and heard everything and didn't think I could be surprised by Representative Jackson any more. Again, I was wrong. After I lost in 2010, the position of Illinois Department Of Transportation Secretary opened up. US Secretary of Transportation, Ray LaHood and I happened to be talking about something unrelated and the issue of IDOT Secretary came up. He thought I would be a great choice for that position and offered to call the Governor on my behalf and so did US Senator Dick Durbin. Many others joined in the call for me to be appointed by the Governor for this important position because I had been involved in transportation issues for all of my years in elected office. I was honored that people thought I would make a good fit. The position had not even been offered to me but when Congressman Jackson heard there was discussion going on with regards to the IDOT Director position he put out a scathing press release detailing how it would be a slap in the face to the residents of the state of Illinois to appoint someone as unqualified as me to such as important position. The governor immediately became nervous with this discourse and that was the end of the IDOT Director discussion.

I suppose actions by members of Congress should not surprise us, given various highly publicized shenanigans over the years but I have to admit I was taken aback to learn that Jesse Jackson, Jr., who represented the district adjoining mine which included portions of south Chicago had misled members of Congress about the proposed South Suburban Airport. He had been claiming the facility was being planned for *his* district. I guess if you say something long enough you begin to believe it yourself but Will County, where the airport had been on the drawing board for more than twenty-five years, even before Jackson had served in Congress was not in his district at all but in mine. Before I was in Congress, the proposed project fell within my state legislative district. Yet Jackson had falsely stated to members of the House Transportation Committee, in his one minute speeches on numerous times from the floor of Congress and during evening special orders that the proposed airport was being planned for his district. I recall the look of amazement on the face of Representative John Olver (D-MA), a member of the Appropriation Transportation Subcommittee, when I told him that Jackson's development group was trying to get FAA support for a third Chicago airport in a district he did not represent. Congressman Dave Obey (D-WI) who was Chairman of Appropriations just shook his head when I mentioned it to him. He said he wasn't surprised by any of Jackson's antics. Many members I talked to said they ignored his regular rants because they never amounted to anything anyway and it wasn't worth getting "into it" with him. Ignoring him is what has made Jackson more dangerous and exactly what has allowed him to get out of hand.

I support the South Suburban Airport under conditions that it would be run by a duly constituted local airport authority like any other airport in the United States. The plan Jackson had been pushing for fifteen years was legally under the control of two North Suburban mayors who came up with the idea of a South Suburban Airport to stop expansion of Chicago O'Hare Airport into their communities. With assistance of the late US Representative Henry Hyde, the two mayors obtained funding to explore development of an airport in Will County fifty miles south of Chicago. They built a bipartisan coalition with Jackson who arranged for his Chief of Staff, Rick Bryant to also serve as Executive Director of an entity known as the Abraham Lincoln National Airport Company (ALNAC). The two men enlisted the support of South Suburban Mayors from his district to join ALNAC with promises of jobs and economic benefits. The towns had to pay a fee of anywhere from $10,000 to $25,000 each to join his "plan." Those promises of jobs and economic benefits have never come to fruition and many are very angry that they haven't seen those benefits.

SNC Lavalin and LCOR are the developers that the congressman has had under contract for many years. Unfortunately, for the constituents who live in Illinois-2 they believe Jackson when he repeats over and over again that the governor has $700 million sitting on his desk for the airport and he should release it. First of all, the governor does not have $700 million sitting on his desk and second, if he did he should be paying long-overdue bills with it.

The problem was two mayors from communities fifty miles away still had legal control over the airport development entity. Will County leaders who are in complete control of the permitting process were not going to cede control of development in their own county to a couple of small suburban mayors who were only concerned with stopping the expansion of O'Hare. It's ironic these mayors wanted to do the very same thing to the South Suburban area that they are now fighting and complaining that Chicago was doing to them with regard to O'Hare: not allowing them a say in what was going on in their community. Illinois Attorney General, Lisa Madigan, ruled against the commission on the basis that ALNAC's development organization was in violation of home rule. ALNAC had to redo their commission bylaws cutting out all towns that were not home rule.

After his election to the US Senate, Obama tried in 2005 to broker a power sharing agreement between Jackson's group and those who represented Will County. Larry Walsh was a state Senator but left in 2004 when he became Will County Executive. Just as we were about to discuss our suggestions for a power sharing agreement, Jesse Jackson, Jr. spoke directly to Obama and mentioned that he had been considering running for US Senate himself but had stepped aside to accommodate Obama who was clearly startled at this political gamesmanship. The tenor of the meeting which was supposed to be about rolling up our sleeves and working out an agreement point by point had changed. The session was to be private to facilitate negotiations and was held at the University of Chicago campus in Hyde Park. It did not go well because Jackson refused to negotiate and Obama has never been able to fully embrace it. Larry Walsh and I went ahead and outlined our ideas designed to meet Jackson half way, but Representative Jackson and his Chief of Staff/Executive Director of ALNAC Rick Bryant were opposed to anything we suggested. I was not at all surprised when Obama chose not to convene any more meetings on the airport seeing what a waste of time it would be.

Emil Jones also held what he had hoped would be a productive negotiating session between Larry Walsh, myself and the congressman. We all agreed within that meeting that when we walked out of the room we would not talk to the press while our negotiations moved forward. We walked out of Emil's office in the Thompson Center to a flood of reporters and most of us kept our word. The congressman on the other hand proceeded to talk to the press on exactly what we talked about and how it wouldn't work. It was the end of discussions again.

Senator Larry Walsh was very close to Barack Obama since serving together in the Illinois state Senate and visited the Senator in Washington, DC, quite often. They would visit in Obama's office while the Senator would have his lunch. Walsh appreciated the time with Obama and would often ask for a staff member to sit in during these airport discussions because of the need for another ear and someone to take notes. Even during the primary election between Jackson and myself in 2012, it was the only thing the congressman had to talk about and he dug his heels in even further. I heard him on Cliff Kelly's popular African American radio station WVON 1690AM say that he would "never relinquish control to anyone who had ever disagreed or fought him" on his ALNAC plan for an airport. I think that says it all.

When I negotiated a project that needed to get done—Centerpoint Intermodal—I brought everyone into my office and no one left until we got it done. This was a project that created over 5,000 jobs. No one got everything they wanted but the project got done. It is so much easier to accomplish things when you do not have a personal agenda.

As I traveled the district during the primary election I never realized what a bone of contention the airport was to the northern part of Illinois-2. First of all they were tired of hearing about this airport that never seemed to materialize and wasn't even in Jackson's district and second if jobs ever did become available at the airport site forty miles away there was no public transportation for them to get to the job site. The Red Line which is part of the Chicago Transit Authority (CTA) ended at ninety-fifth street.

Census and Redisricting of Congressional Seats

You may not realize how much is affected by the census form you fill out every ten years but one of the results is redistricting of all 435 congressional districts. In Illinois we gained in population but not at the rate as other states so we lost one seat and Illinois will be going from nineteen to eighteen seats. In the past decade, the Chicagoland region lost more than 200,000 people. The Democrats who controlled the map drawing process had to do three things: they had to draw three districts to accommodate the sitting Congressmen in Chicago, find each of them about 70,000 residents and keep them all a majority minority. In order to do that, each congressional district had to stretch well into the suburbs. If the Republicans would have had control of drawing the map they may have eliminated one of the city congressional seats and made the suburban congressional seats more powerful. In past years when one party didn't control everything the control of the map was done by a coin toss.

Illinois Senate President John Cullerton met with Nancy Pelosi who gave him her blessing when it came to drawing the map for all Illinois districts. After the map was drawn, Jesse signed off and John said Representative Jackson was perfectly happy. Senate President Cullerton told me he was flabbergasted when Jackson decided to side with the Republican's in their suit against the map drawn by the Democrats; the same map Jackson just a few months earlier approved of. Speculation of me entering the race is what many said accounted for his change of heart when it came to removing his support of the newly drawn Illinois-2.

I was in Springfield to attend a State Central Committeeman meeting and happened to confront Speaker Madigan about what the plan was for redistricting the congressional districts especially Illinois-2 which is that of Congressman Jesse Jackson, Jr. I had heard that the Illinois-2 would be stretched south into the old Illinois-11. Speaker Madigan looked me straight in the eye and said "We needed to find almost 100,000 people for Congressman Jackson's district and we couldn't move him east, because Lake Michigan is in the way." So I looked at him with a jaundiced eye and responded "Well, I guess you stopped me from ever running again." He smiled as he walked away. In May the Illinois Legislature passed the bill which included the new congressional districts. I am sure Mr. Jackson was jumping for joy because finally the possible third Chicago Airport that he had been working on for fifteen years would be in Illinois-2, not Illinois-11.

Come summer, my phone started ringing off the hook, with people telling me I had to run against Congressman Jackson in the primary. I would look at the phone, tell them they were crazy and hang up. Instead of slowing down the calls increased so I figured I better think about getting into this primary.

Possible Run for Congress

Senator Dick Durbin's words from 2008 were ringing in my ears at this point. I remember him telling me that you need to think long and hard about what is the right decision for you and your family but once you make that decision don't ever look back but to move forward. Senator Durbin has been not only a great friend he has been a wonderful US Senator for Illinois. He is fair and considerate of the people in Illinois. You may not agree with him but he doesn't walk away from anyone. We traveled together while I was in Congress and he always took the time to answer any and all questions to explain what was behind his reasoning for a vote. His ability to articulate any issue has always amazed me.

I called former Senate President Emil Jones. I had seen him earlier in the summer at pool party at a friend's house. I asked him what he thought about getting people together to discuss the pros and cons of running for Congress. We met the next evening at E & B Restaurant that he owned with his best buddy Bill Williams. The room was packed with political operatives who thought it was a great idea and were ready to help me. The first thing Emil said was I needed to hire Sean Howard; someone who knew everyone and was sharp as a tack and I found that to be true. I took his advice and within a few days we had a start on meetings with people I needed to know and people who needed to know me.

My Entrance Into the Race for Congress

By September, I put my team together and on October 6, 2011 announced my run for Congress when it became evident that Jackson would be running unopposed in a new district that included my home. Many people got on board quickly, petitions were printed and we were off and running. I still had an office and a couple hundred thousand dollars in my campaign bank account. I set a goal to raise a couple hundred thousand more. Raising campaign money had never been hard for me, I raised millions while in Congress. This should be a piece of cake based on all the people who had contributed before, and those who had recently called me and said they wanted to help. Nothing could have been further from the truth.

I did my announcement on October 6, 2011, across the street from my Alma Mater, Bloom High School, in Chicago Heights. It was great to have so many friends, family and supporters there.

Every TV Station, radio and newspaper person attended and it wasn't so much about me, even though I was the first big name to go against the congressman since 1995, but it was about Jesse Jackson, Jr. and how they haven't been able to catch up with him in more than three years. Now that he had his first real challenge since 1995 the talk was whether he would reappear?

The Pastors Played a Big Part in the Election

One person who attended that I haven't seen since my Illinois state Senate days was Reverend Tyrone Crider. He asked if I would stick around for a few minutes afterwards because he needed to talk to me about getting a meeting together. He wanted me to know that he and Apostle Carl White had a group of Pastors that wanted to meet with me. They were tired of Jackson and were so excited to hear I was running against him because they knew me, they had a good history with me and knew I delivered from my days as Illinois Senator. We had that meeting of about ten to fifteen pastors within a week that went so well I was handed a contract by Rev. Crider of all the things they were going to do for me as well as the amount of money it was going to cost me each month. In fact, Rev. Crider expected his first check that day. I don't know too many people who get paid before they do anything but I paid a few days later because I was advised by Sean that's how it is done. In fact Sean said I would have fainted if I saw the original amount they wanted from me before Sean negotiated them down.

Every month before I wrote the check I would continually ask for a report of their activities to no avail. I didn't think I was asking too much. The only thing I ever received was a phone call from the bank wondering if he was who he said he was because he went directly to my bank where the check was written. I was told everyone takes their check to the bank the check was written on to cash so they don't have to claim the income on their taxes, because there is no way to track it. I was speechless. It may be true with people who don't keep good records but not someone like me with a very detailed compliance officer.

Eventually when I didn't get anything for my money I was told that I would get my name mentioned in the *Gospel Tribune* church newspapers that Rev. Crider was charge of. It came in the form of Meet The Candidate in a corner of page twenty. Oh well, I didn't think I could learn any more lessons, but they just kept coming. The money I was spending was becoming defense not offense. The only answers I could ever get is it's better than what they would do to you if you didn't give them the money. In my opinion extortion, blackmail and shakedown are all words that come to mind when I think about what was going on throughout this campaign.

Falsehoods

Mr. Jackson was able to use his considerable speaking ability to spread outright falsehoods to confuse people about my record. Outrageously in one commercial he claimed I voted against the *Patient Protection and Affordable Health Care Act* but then in another commercial portrayed me as blaming the President for my loss in 2010 to Tea Party opponent Adam Kinzinger because I did support the Act. Obviously he knew I was deeply involved in the passage of the *PPACA*. I was proud to support it. He was able to get Cogresswomen Corrine Brown (D-FL) and Maxine Waters (D-CA) to do radio commercials for African American radio that many thought were condescending and racist.

Jackson's campaign also told *Crain's Chicago Business* "Congresswoman Halvorson wants people to believe that she's a progressive Democrat, but she votes like a conservative Republican." The congressman did everything to portray me as the Republican in our campaign like we were running in a general election, not a primary. The Congressional Quarterly showed that I had supported the President's positions ninety percent of the time while Jackson had supported him eighty percent of the time. Jackson's claim was based on the deliberately misleading claim that I had voted eighty-eight times "against the President." Out of more than 1700 votes as a congresswoman I had voted against the *Democrat Leadership* eighty-eight times, not the President. However, Jackson and his communication team of Kitty Kurth and Kevin Lampe went to great lengths to confuse the voters even calling me the Republican in the race. Jackson hired pollster Celinda Lake, a leading Democrat strategist on women's issues who worked with organizations like Emily's list. I was told it was Celinda who was able to keep Emily's List from endorsing me after they had overwhelmingly supported me in 2008 and 2010. According the their website: "E.M.I.L.Y.'s List is dedicated to electing pro-choice Democratic women to office. E.M.I.L.Y.'s List looks for viable political opportunities and recruits strong pro-choice Democratic women candidates to run." E.M.I.L.Y. is the acronym for Early Money Is Like Yeast. I love the name and I love what the organization set out to do but over the years they have gotten so big that they have moved from their mission described in the first sentence above to their second sentence of opportunity as most important. It is not about being dedicated to electing pro-choice Democratic women to office anymore unless it is a *viable political opportunity* for them. So as I list some of my disappointments I would have to add the hypocrisy of women's groups not standing up for a former member of Congress who happens to be a woman against a Congressman who is being investigated by the US House Ethics Committee for corruption. Why else would they turn their back on someone they had supported in 2008, 2010 and had encouraged me to run again until I was a candidate against Jesse Jackson Jr. It is unfortunate at a time when we need more women running and winning at all levels of elected office being a woman was not enough for some organizations.

Comparison of our Records

A straightforward comparison of our respective records should have persuaded the party leadership at all levels to at least stay neutral. In sixteen years, eight terms of office as a congressman, Jackson passed only two bills. One of these bills was to name a post office and another was a routine bill to honor Abraham Lincoln.

By contrast, in the two years that I served in Congress, I sponsored eleven jobs bills, a number of which became part of larger bills that eventually passed and helped ease the recession by enabling small businesses to hire new employees. Jackson talked about jobs and I delivered jobs: more than 5000 by brokering an agreement to expand the Intermodal transportation facility in Will County. That was just one project.

Also, it was hard to understand how Jackson voted against the interests of his own constituents by opposing the Hire Act, a jobs bill I helped write and was honored to be invited to the bill signing for. I was also dismayed, but not surprised to learn when I joined him in Congress that he had been misleading members of the House by telling them that the plans for a South Suburban Airport was located in his district when in fact the proposed site was in mine. Members of the House Transportation Committee as well as the Appropriation Subcommittee for Transportation were dumbfounded when I explained this them.

Democrat Leadership

Apparently none of this mattered very much to the Democratic leadership when I challenged Jesse. Party leaders and elected officials routinely support the incumbent. It is easier and they don't want to rock the boat or bring real change that would bring power closer to the regular people instead of the party apparatus. Everyone wants to take the easy way out, avoid confrontation—even if they know it isn't the best thing for the people. Besides, it costs money and forces people to think and make choices instead of just doing what your mayor or your committeeman tell you to do. To the people who don't listen to the committeeman or the mayor, you probably don't vote in primaries anyway so no one worries about you. If you do vote, it isn't in a primary where all the major elections are decided. At least in Illinois red districts are redder and blue districts are bluer. Its just the way it is. Unfortunately, those who don't like to vote in primaries are stuck with whom a small percentage of the electorate select.

So why is it that someone such as myself, who was Illinois Senate Majority Leader; who has a proven record of serving constituents, is a team player and a good Democrat, gets defeated by such a huge margin in the primary? Not because I wouldn't have been a good congresswoman, but because the leadership of the district was afraid of change. I was told all the time they didn't like the incumbent congressman but they had no choice. They secretly wished me luck but they had gotten things from Jackson's office and a few told me they were warned they would never get anything again if they didn't publicly endorse him. I completely understood. These guys were AFRAID. But when seniors start telling me they have to vote for Jr because if they don't they would be cut off from their Medicare and Social Security there is a real problem. I received a call from a lady who wanted to vote for me but said she couldn't because Jesse would "know" and then she would be cut off from her benefits. Try as I may I couldn't get her and others to understand that Social Security and Medicare were not something a member of Congress could cut off. We all have a choice. Some people just aren't strong enough to stand up and make that choice. Those who stayed home and there were a lot, enabled that process. No one can complain you don't want a certain person in office if you are not willing to do what it takes to CHANGE. Staying home and not voting in primaries is not going to work anymore.

Thornton Township

The story of one local politician named Frank Zuccarelli says a lot about why so many people say they are tired of political games. The year I was elected township clerk (1993) was the same year Frank Zuccarelli was elected Township Supervisor of Thornton Township. I became a state Senator in 1996 and represented Thornton Township. Even in 2002 when redistricting happened and I was moved farther south and no longer represented Thornton Township I still attended many of Frank's events to support him. In 2008 when elected to Congress I was moved even further south and now represented over 700,000 people instead of 200,000. It was a bit difficult to do much of anything outside of my own district. I had eight counties and people wanted to see me.

When I did see Frank or any of Thornton Township leadership they would complain about Congressman Jackson. When I was contemplating running for Congress, I repeatedly called Frank Zuccarelli and left many messages to get his support. I even went to the Township building in person: no Frank. Despite his often expressed disappointment with Representative Jackson, however, Frank would never call me back. I went to his meetings many of which he wasn't even in attendance himself. His chief guy, Don Manning would tell me "you know Frank, he'll do what he can for you, but. . . ." So finally Frank was at one of his own meetings and announced that they were endorsing Jesse because they hadn't heard from me. He said "She is a nice girl, fun to party with, but she's never around anymore." They were going with Jesse. He had done so much for them. He had no idea I was in the room because he doesn't visit with anyone before the meeting starts. In fact, he gets "announced" and just walks on stage. When someone on the stage told him I was sitting in the front row practically in front of him, he acknowledged me and brushed me off by saying "oh, Debbie I didn't see you sitting there. Feel free to pass your stuff out to the people when the meeting is over." It was like Frank Zuccarelli enjoyed being a bully. Kyle Kasparek a wonderful young man who was running for state representative, involved in the young dems was sitting in the front row with his supporters all in matching "Kyle Kasparek for State Rep" shirts. It was shocking to watch as Kyle was castigated from the podium by Frank asking where Kyle had been over the years because Frank hadn't seen financial support or otherwise from him, no attendance at his meeting etc. How dare Kyle come to an organization thinking he could get support from the all-powerful Z-Team. Now if you were a young person would you want to be involved in politics ever again? To be embarrassed not only in front of your friends but in front of Frank's dwindling organization? This is a time to be encouraging our young people to get involved in politics. They are our future. He did the same thing to Donna Miller who was running for state Senator. At least she wasn't blindsided by him and I am sure it was because he disliked Donna's husband David Miller. Frank glowed as he went through the exercises of putting people down. By the next morning I received so many calls and emails about how they disagreed with Frank but said, "that was just Frank." How sad for Thornton Township.

Bloom Township

The same thing happened in Bloom Township. Bloom Township languished for years getting no federal attention because in 1995 Bloom Township supported Emil Jones over Jackson in the special election for Congress. Terry Mathews, Bloom Township Committeeman felt Jackson had held a grudge all those years because of the lack of support for Jackson. So when people heard Jackson was coming to a Bloom Township meeting, it was a big deal. I was born and raised, attended school and represented Bloom Township for twelve years as Senator. I was accessible and supported everything they did. The only time I did not represent Bloom Township was the two years I served in Congress. When we heard Jackson was going to address a Bloom Township meeting, my supporters were excited to finally have a chance to ask questions of the elusive member of Congress who had not been accessible to people in Bloom Township in years. The night of the big meeting Jackson arrived late to a room of about twenty people. He came in, sat in the front row, spoke to no one individually because he was on his phone the entire time. When he was introduced he spoke about the need to reelect Barack Obama, took no questions and walked out the side door. After he left Matthews told the audience "This is who you WILL work for" and abruptly adjourned the meeting. He was obviously perturbed that people at the meeting had questions for the Congressman. I was disappointed that the decision was made to support someone who had not been around, who had no interest in engaging with anyone. It isn't like he was running against just anyone. I was from there, I had represented them, and I cared. But I didn't even get a chance to make my case.

The reason I bring these two committeemen stories up is because they are a couple more of my disappointments for the people. We need to be encouraging people to be involved in political organizations not turning them away. No one goes to the meetings and it is hard to get election day workers. This happens in both parties and isn't just a Democratic party thing. Don't complain—you let it happen when you don't get involved. These are the people making all the decisions because so few people are taking the time to vote or go to their local township meetings. I agree we are all busy raising children and working. Find someone who does attend and get information from them regarding what is going on.

Does It Really Matter Who Relates Better to the People

When I told *Chicago Sun-Times* Columnist Laura Washington about all the African-Americans who said they were going to vote for me and we were getting past the race issue she said to me, "Don't you think they are just being polite?" I didn't know what to say because that hadn't even occurred to me until election night when that proved to be true.

Jesse has a home on the Southside of Chicago but he grew up in DC and went to school at St. Albans where Al Gore, Dan Quayle and many other famous people in DC attended. I on the other hand have been a lifelong resident of the district, grew up on free and reduced lunch programs and was a single mom. I strongly identified with so many of the people I had hoped to represent. Could it be that I was someone the people of the district could relate to until . . . they forgot about Martin Luther Kings' speech: . . .won't be judged on the color of my skin but the content of my character?

Michael Taylor

I met quite a few people eager to make a buck off me on the campaign trail but the one who stands out is Michael Taylor of Kankakee, son of James Taylor publisher of the *City News* and Republican candidate for Congress in Illinois-2. He would call me everyday asking me to give him money so they could take cameras around and listen to complaints about Jackson. I told him I wanted no part in any shaky scheme he had up his sleeve. Plus I had no money at this point to do any advertising. Michael Taylor felt I was being disrespectful to him and his father for not supporting them.They wanted to be treated like any other business owner would be. Other than his dad's newspaper in Kankakee, Michael had several radio and cable TV shows. He wanted $10,000. I about choked on my Wheaties but I gave him an "A" for persistence. I told him once I decided to advertise I would include him in the budget. That wasn't good enough and he continued to call. I told him I would put him in touch with my campaign attorney who would work out the details if and when I decided to do anything but he might as well get the $10,000 figure out of his head right now. He was noticeably angry with me. The attorney got back to me and said they put together a very good contract for advertising for $2500 and of course Michael Taylor needed the money that day before he would start anything. My husband's very sensitive B.S. meter was going off and I was skeptical but we were told "Write the check, this is how it's done in the neighborhood." I wrote the check and Michael Taylor immediately went to cash the check at my bank. The normal procedure when someone went directly to the bank to cash their check was for someone from the bank to call us to verify their identity. On the day we were going to do the TV show to record the commercials for his radio show, Michael Taylor cancelled but not with us but with our attorney. We were five minutes away from his studio. He gave some silly reason about me attending a Republican meeting asking for crossover votes. I had no idea what that was about but I believe it had nothing to do with the reason I was given. The Taylor's were good at telling you what would happen if you didn't "advertise" with them. Usually the candidate that gave the most money got the *City News* endorsement. Here is the kicker. No future recordings would be done without more money. I never received anything for the first $2500. Needless to say, we couldn't get our original $2500 back and I sure wasn't going to be stupid enough to give them any more money. These are people who wanted to be treated like the other businesses and get the respect they felt they deserved. The readers of this book get to decide whether they deserve respect as a business.

The Great People I Met

I spent every weekend in different parts of the city and met the greatest people. I loved how many communities still have their Saturday night church dances and potluck dinners and every Alderman in the city has such pride in their ward and were so gracious to share it with me. Standing outside of the grocery stores talking to everyone, listening to their concerns was enlightening because I haven't cornered the market on good ideas. I visited many of the schools in the communities and some were beautiful like Gwendolyn Brooks College Prep in the Roseland neighborhood and some were in terrible shape. There was great disparity.

Roseland has been in the press recently because there have been eight homicides this year in the police district that includes the Roseland neighborhood on the South Side, compared to four at the same time last year according to the Chicago Police Department. Roseland Community Hospital is partnering with local churches to speak out against gun violence with Arms Around Roseland. However, I also want to share how the residents love their neighborhood and are spending time and effort to make it safer. Roseland is located on the far South Side of Chicago, a great community with many longtime homeowners. Roseland is also fortunate to be home to historic landmarks like the West Pullman area whose signature red brick homes can be found throughout the far

Southeast side of Roseland. Pullman has been featured in several major motion pictures. *Road to Perdition* (Tom Hanks, Paul Newman) was filmed in historic Pullman, showing the factory and how it "once was" with workers, as well as many other scenes of the neighborhood itself. The 1993 film *The Fugitive* had several key scenes in Pullman, as this was where the one armed man lived in the movie. You can see Harrison Ford in a local bar using the pay phone, then he runs down the alley, then atop many of the Pullman rowhouses. In April 2007, Universal Studios began filming of "The Express" which also features several scenes in Pullman, one which includes the cast leaving the Greenstone Church (see Ernie Davis). *The Polar Express* (Robert Zemeckis, Tom Hanks) movie visuals the North Pole were based on Pullman architecture. The building Santa Claus comes out of is the Pullman Company Administration Building is based on the town of Pullman. Gwendolyn Brooks College Preparatory Academy, a magnet school in Roseland which recently received a silver medal ranking in the 2010 US News and World Report evaluation of the best high schools in the nation. This ranking was based on data analyzed from 21,000 high schools nationwide. That is just one of the neighborhoods tucked away in Illinois-2 that deserves representation. Neighborhoods such as Roseland and towns like Riverdale, Harvey, Phoenix and Dixmoor need help. They need someone who is going to make sure there is someone in Washington fighting for the resources necessary to keep the streets safe, police officers ever present and the schools the best they can be.

I didn't like speaking at forums alone but I had no choice, the congressman wouldn't show up. He didn't think he needed to be there to answer to the voters. As it turned out he was right, no one really cared if he was there or not. Other than the *Chicago Tribune* Editorial Board, Jesse refused to be in the same room as I was and didn't answer to the people. Saturday mornings I visited at least four or five restaurants to meet enough people for my liking. I was in my element. Give me a room to work and I was happy.

Between October and March, I only missed church twice: Christmas and New Years both fell on a Sunday. My husband and I attended ninety-seven church services. Some had as many as 10,000 people in attendance and one church had only six people at their service. I enjoyed meeting and going to them all. I danced, donated and sang my heart out at each service no matter how many parishioners each church had. I not only appreciated the opportunity to attend, the majority of them were the highlight of my week. Most churches expected nothing from me except to share their service with me and those who were there couldn't have been more gracious. I tried to arrange my schedule each week so I could stay for the entire service. Many times I returned for another service. The choirs were great, the Pastor's message made a difference in my life and I believe I am a better person because of all the people I met.

There were many pastors who were there for me and let me speak at their church, some may have been with the congressman but still introduced me if I was visiting that Sunday. I want to personally thank those who were with me and stayed with me. I am sure it was hard not to give in when Jackson tried to buy them off. A special shout out to those of you who put yourselves on the front line for me such as Bishop Larry Trotter, Pastor Keith Williams, Bishop Lance Davis, Pastor Ronnie Lee, and Pastor Anthony Williams.

However, in a campaign, you will always find people that put a sour taste in your mouth, users who tell you what they think you want to hear, but fail to stand up and be counted. On occasion there were those who would say as you were leaving the church "make sure and write a big check before you leave." I guess it takes all kinds.

Satanic Force

In February, Jesse Jackson, Jr. got together with some of *his* ministers in University Park. They held a press conference on the congressman's behalf that quickly became a rally saying my running for Congress was that of a satanic force. A group of pastors had never called me the devil before: at least not that I knew of. I had to shake my head to think a group of reverends who preach on Sunday about God and his love for others would refer to me as the "devil" just because I chose to oppose him in the election to give people a choice.

Emil Jones' Endorsement

Things were going great and the endorsements were rolling in but everyone was still waiting for former Senate President Emil Jones to give the nod that he was going to stand with me to do the formal endorsement. Popular Illinois Secretary of State, Jesse White, a respected African American that I worked with in the state legislature signaled he wanted to endorse me but he too was waiting for Jones. Alderman Carrie Austin (also State Central Committeewoman of the 2nd district) and Commissioner Debra Simms had already endorsed me but were waiting for Jones, to formally stand with me at the press conference we were planning. The date was finally chosen and a room at the Allegro Hotel in Chicago was rented. Other than the names already mentioned, many more mayors, commissioners and committeemen were going to be in attendance. We had been trying to get Jones to pick a date for the press conference for six months but Jones was worried about his son, Emil III getting a primary opponent because he was "taking sides" in my race. Once filing deadline passed and it was no longer possible for him to have an opponent in the upcoming Democratic primary Alderman Austin had finally gotten him to realize if Emil the III was going to get a challenge, it would happen no matter what and we had our date.

We were approaching the Allegro Hotel where the Press Conference was to take place when I received a call from Alderman Carrie Austin telling me that Jones had decided just a moment ago that he couldn't be at the press conference at the Allegro

Hotel and stand before the cameras to endorse me. Alderman Austin was HOT when she called me. She apologized that he couldn't call me himself. I told her I didn't expect him to. He never could give bad news himself. It was no different than our days in the Senate together when he sent a messenger to deliver news to me that I could be removed from the Rules Committee [if I didn't behave]. She had plenty of four-letter words for him and I don't blame her. Putting together a press conference takes a lot of planning. She assured me that he would be there tomorrow. Supposedly it was an emergency, at least that is what the press was told. Carrie calmly told me to turn around, go home and reschedule the press conference for tomorrow—a day that never came.

I will never know why Emil Jones, Jr. who came up to me one evening in 1996 to tell me I was a perfect candidate to be a Senator who was *going places* never did call to tell me why he couldn't just stand with me to tell the public why I would be the better person to represent Illinois-2. I am left to wonder and imagine. I have been told so many different things but the one that makes the most sense is Emil just didn't want to be known as the African American who stood up for a white woman from the suburbs against another African American. We could have saved a lot of time, effort, phone calls and meetings had he just told me that in the beginning. He will never know how crushed I was because I don't believe in friends leaving other friends hanging. I guess that call will never come.

Race

There needs to be an honest discussion about race. A white professor told me about a situation he encountered when he wanted to teach a class on Diversity and Race. He was told the class would have to be taught by an African American, not a white man. I asked him why and he said, "No minority would attend my class, I have tried it already." He would not share many of the details because he was still visibly shaken that he had been told he knew nothing about what it was like to be a minority and it would be an insult to think he could teach a class on diversity or race. We need to get away from the "talk" and get to "policy".

How about supporting policies and people that are good to lift all people out of racial inequalities. While I was getting my Bachelor's Degree at Governors State University I took a class called Dealing with Diversity. I loved that class and wish we could mandate it in Junior High School. It is never too early to teach about our similarities instead of our differences. However, I don't think it is our children we have trouble with, it is our adults.

More Surprises to Come

I couldn't believe one night when I turned on the evening news news and right there before my eyes who was having a press conference in support of Jesse Jackson Jr.?

None other than Reverend Tyrone Crider, Apostle Carl White and some of the other Pastors who met with me early on in my campaign telling me they wanted to help me because Jackson had been unresponsive. Carl White was the one actually speaking saying that they were endorsing Jesse Jackson, Jr.

To learn that I had been used by those I thought of as my spiritual leaders was like getting knocked in the head with a hammer. I had already been kicked in the stomach by Emil Jones. These were the Pastors who brought me in very early and stood with me in their churches. I think about it now and how it was such a well thought out plan by some who never planned on supporting me. How better to get to Jackson than to support someone else and hold that over his head until he came through with something for them. I can't believe I fell for it. Allegedly, the congressman was told he could get the pastors back by writing them into a grant already promised to a local health consortium. It was too good to pass up.

I went to a church in South Holland the Sunday before the March primary and as I was about to sit down in the pew I couldn't believe what I saw: the latest edition of the *Gospel Tribune*. You will never guess who's picture was on the front page, bigger than life: Jesse Jackson, Jr. This, from the same pastors who told me they were tired of his antics because he never did anything for him, that he took them for granted. I guess they finally got something from him.

In early March Nancy Pelosi came out to Operation Push to endorse Jackson. I give her credit for calling me the day before to tell me about her plans and that she had no choice. I told her everyone has a choice but she said she had to do this. At the press conference where busloads of people were brought in, Pelosi said just a few words about his seniority and did not take any questions. [I wonder how much that seniority is doing for the district now that he has been away from Congress on medical leave for the last three months.] Have you noticed a pattern of no accountability to the voters? Not once has anyone been allowed to ask a question of the congressman. I received about twenty new volunteers and ninety new sign locations once people saw the coverage of that endorsement.

I did get help from a nonpartisan SuperPAC. This particular SuperPAC went after Democrats as well as Republicans. The Houston based group called Campaign for Primary Accountability went against Republican Congressman Don Manzullo in favor of my former opponent Adam Kinzinger and was successful in that race. Their purpose was to defeat members of Congress they felt had been in congress too long, had become ineffective and had serious primary challengers.

Election Night

Election night, March 20, 2012 Jim and I turned on the television when the polls closed when we realized we had done everything we could. This had been a very strange election. As we had done for years, we started handicapping the races. There were only a few primary races around the state. Both Jim and I felt Tammy Duckworth would win the race in the 8th district against Raja Krishnamoothi. Raja had just ran in the Democratic primary race for state treasurer and narrowly lost. One of the other races was My former opponent Congressman Adam Kinzinger against longtime Congressman Don Manzullo. I thought Manzullo would win even though it would be close. I was very wrong in that race. Kinzinger won big. But the primary race between Jesse Jackson, Jr and I was the big one.There were days when I thought I could never win and then there were days when I thought I could never lose. Never did I think it would turn out the way it did with me getting only thirty percent of the vote.

Tribune Columnists, Clarence Page and John Kass were guests on WGN for their election night coverage. When my race came up, John Kass growled, "that isn't even a race" but then proceeded to talk about all of Jesse Jackson, Jr.'s ethical problems and why didn't the media make a bigger deal out of his problems. When it was brought up to Kass on why didn't he do more, he said that he was just a columnist and they can only do so much by writing columns but he was hoping someone would have dug into Jesse Jackson, Jr's corruption allegations.

Early on primary night it was easy to see that I wasn't going to win Jim and I went to the Fifth Quarter restaurant in Homewood where our supporters were waiting for us. As we approached we noticed that every TV station had their satellites reaching tall into the sky for the evening. I don't think the small town of Homewood has ever seen so much excitement.

As I explained to the audience in my speech, we didn't fail. We may have lost an election, but we still won. We won because we gave the people a choice, and hopefully made the congressman a little stronger and better at his job by making him campaign for the first time since getting elected in 1995. Most people who lose an election will not say this, but for someone who thought they were strong, had thick skin and could stand up to anyone, this experience taught me you are never done learning and getting better at who you are. Because of this election I will be even better at standing up for myself and I will continue to teach others that you can disagree without being disagreeable.

Maybe this campaign didn't make him stronger or a better congressman because within a few short months he had taken a medical leave of absence from Congress for exhaustion and mood disorder.

Now that I have written about the race everyone has asked me to write about I am happy to close this chapter in my life. I am anxious to encourage whoever is the Congressman from Illinois-2 to work both sides of the aisle. Sandy Jackson was wrong when she said Congress is in Washington not Chicago. The constituents that the Congressman needs to be serving are in Illinois not in Washington. If he does decide to resign and move on, I am praying for him and his family that he finds something that truly makes him happy.

I encourage our leaders to put their own interests aside to do what is in the best interest of the people.

Our country needs to come together or we will never again achieve the greatness of our past.

If women are to succeed in their goals and in changing the political process, they need to stand their ground when necessary. Women who show strength will often become targets, but that is part of the process and to be successful you need to accept some slings and arrows sometimes. It will be ok. Just keep moving forward.

That is why I refer to this quote from Eleanor Roosevelt quite often: The future belongs to those who believe in the beauty of their dreams

13

Where Do We Go From Here?

The future depends on what you do today.
—Mahatma Gandhi

This book is being written as President Obama is heading into the final stage of his reelection campaign. I will share some final thoughts on the political scene I've been part of and also why I think it is absolutely crucial that women get more deeply involved in the political process. I have major concerns about the hyper-partisanship of recent years and the flood of special interest money that now threatens to drown out the voices of the average citizen. My experiences as Illinois Senate Majority Leader and as a member of the US House of Representatives give me hope that our democratic system has the ability to tackle the crucial challenges ahead.

As a member of Congress there were a number of times I disagreed with President Obama's strategy even as I support and applaud his successful efforts to bring affordable health care to our citizens, legislation to curb the worst abuses of the financial sector and to improve services for veterans and women. I am supporting the President's reelection, but I do so hoping that difficult lessons from the first term have been learned and will be taken into account going forward.

An excellent analysis by reporters Sam Stein and Ryan Grim of the *Huffington Post* details how President Obama lost momentum and used up much of his political capital by seeking to play the insider game with a Republican leadership that decided early on not to support any legislation that would improve the president's chance for reelection. They point out that the major changes in government policy set in motion by Franklin Delano Roosevelt and Lyndon Johnson—two masters of the inside game–would never have succeeded if they had not also drummed up strong public support for their legislative efforts. Obama was swept into office with a strong mandate for fixing things like a financial system that had broken down. He also had a list of thirteen million email addresses that could have been mobilized to support efforts to pass health care with a public option as well as jobs creation bills that would have been equal to the dire condition that the country found itself with an economy in free fall. However, instead of mobilizing his vast grass roots network and using the bully pulpit of the Presidency to build public support for his legislative proposals the President sought to make deals with a Republican leadership who blocked him at every turn.

Former Republican Chairman Michael Steele helped engineer the successful midterm elections of 2010 when Republicans captured the House of Representatives. He told *Huffington Post*:

> "We used their [Obama's] model, and what surprised me was *they* stopped using their model. . . I always thought that Obama would actually do both, that he would play the inside game while he was building up the outside strategy of more of a global network that he could pull the trigger on, push a button and, you know, 1,300 people would respond in 10 minutes type thing," said Steele. "I was actually, absolutely surprised. I think they took it for granted. I think they assumed that, 'They love me so much, they'll always be there.' Well, as you know, in this town, love is fleeting. It's a very fickle thing."

Led by the Tea Party, Republican officials decided to ride the wave or get swept under by the Republican minority that became the majority. They could not defeat the health care bill but the Republicans were able to deprive it of a public option that may have driven down health costs even more had it been part of the bill. This victory weakened the President from getting the necessary votes he would need on future issues by allowing the Republicans to pick off a nervous Blue Dog Democrat from time to time.

For a variety of reasons, my fellow freshman members of Congress and I became aware long before either the Obama administration or Nancy Pelosi and Harry Reid, that the President's strategy was creating backlash and resistance in many parts of the country because as newly elected members of marginal districts we returned home every weekend.

On a few occasions I was able to speak to the President during this time and I pressed him to take his case to the public and use his persuasive powers. He responded that his polls indicated the public was still with him and he was in good shape. The President simply didn't see the urgency as I did. Those of us on the ground in our districts could certainly see the way the wind was blowing in the late summer and fall of 2009 and it wasn't in favor of the Obama sponsored legislation. As President of the freshman class I was asked to raise these issues at the regular Wednesday meetings that Nancy Pelosi held for us. On one hand I give The Speaker a lot of credit for making herself available to the freshmen congressional representatives and while we learned a tremendous amount about how leadership viewed the issues meetings became informational only. I thrived on the in depth material and attention to detail but I found the members who didn't attend were the ones who were tired of getting their arms twisted or lectured to.

The Speaker and her leadership team could have benefited by listening to the warnings we gave about discontent from a public that was hearing only grass roots Republican opposition. Instead of heeding these warnings of trouble ahead the Speaker was somewhat dismissive telling us to do a better job of "educating" the people in our districts about the issues. This was something most freshmen representatives were already doing but none of us could begin to match the national megaphone or bully pulpit of the President, who could have guaranteed media coverage of any issue he chose to highlight and explain. The House leadership was frustrated with the backseat mentality that was going on at times also.

Seeking alternatives to what was going on in Washington on issues like the *American Clean Energy and Securities Act,* I tried to persuade top officials of several national environmental groups to contact their members in my district to explain the importance of the energy legislation and counter the vastly inflated claims of costs to industry, but got little response at a time when many industries were financing an all out misleading assault on the "cap and trade" component of the energy bill. We had help in our district from people willing to validate what we were trying to accomplish but the mass amounts of money that was flooding our districts by the Koch brothers who were funding the Tea Party's efforts completely drowned out the grassroots movement and credibility going on. Koch brothers are most notable for their control of Koch Industries, the second largest privately owned company in the United States. The family business was started by Fred C. Koch, who developed a new cracking method for the refinement of heavy oil into gasoline. Fred's four sons litigated against each other over their interests in the business during the 1980s and 1990s. Only the White House would have had the power to focus media attention on the strong arguments in favor of the bill that would benefit the public at minimal cost to industry but that never happened.

Aside from squandering the President's political capital far too early in his first term the decisions to play the inside game took the Barack Obama I knew for many years away from his strengths and diminished his image. He now seemed like just another traditional politician making backroom deals. Without a strong wind at his back from engaged supporters the administration was left to negotiate deals.

Ironically, the affordable health care bill which had languished for months in the Senate and no longer seemed possible to pass began to revive only after outside health care activists pushing to revive it began getting members of the Senate to sign on to show their support. Momentum began to build again. These actions helped force the President back into public forums where he put Republicans on the spot. When the President spoke to Republicans at their Caucus retreat in Baltimore, his aides made sure television cameras were allowed to cover the event as he called out members of the caucus for their knee jerk opposition and intellectual dishonesty. Among other things he pointed out that ideas incorporated in the affordable health care bill which had been endorsed by former Republican leaders such as Robert Dole and Howard Baker were now being portrayed as "radical" and "socialist" by John Boehner's (R-OH) followers in the House. A similar public forum a month later at Blair House gave the administration new momentum that eventually enabled passage of the *Patient Protection and Affordable Care Act,* albeit without the public option which was negotiated away much earlier.

I strongly disagree with those who claim that Obama abandoned his willingness to work across the aisle which was part of his widespread appeal going back to the national attention he received as the keynote speaker at the 2004 Democratic convention. As I said in earlier chapters, from his earliest days in the Illinois Senate he cosponsored key legislation on ethics with Republican leaders like Kirk Dillard. As a US Senator he cosponsored legislation with conservative Senator Tom Coburn. Going back to his days at Harvard Law School he was elected editor of the Law Review because he enjoyed the support of conservatives who appreciated the fact that he took their views into consideration.

By the time Obama took office January of 2009 Republican senior leaders Boehner and McConnell had already decided they would not vote for legislation that might make the President look good and ease his path to reelection. As Republican Senate leader Mitch McConnell told the National Journal, "The single most important thing we want to achieve is for President Obama to be a one-term president." That is surely why during the grave national economic crisis the new administration could not find one single Republican House vote for the stimulus package–a temporary measure which saved and created millions of jobs–according to independent studies. That is why other Obama legislation with wide public support such as Wall Street reform received so little Republican support despite a widespread public understanding that deregulation of the financial industry is what led to the mortgage crisis and that banks needed to be regulated and held accountable for their actions.

Barack Obama's problem was not that he was unwilling to work with Republicans but that he did not recognize early enough that they were unwilling to work with him. Lessons learned? I hope so.

As for the influence of money in politics, the evidence is overwhelming that the Supreme Court's controversial *Citizens United* (5-4) decision has drastically changed the political landscape to the detriment of the average citizen in a democracy. Using an infinitely elastic definition of "free speech," the Supreme Court effectively ruled that "SuperPacs" like Karl Rove's GPS Crossroads can receive unlimited funds from undisclosed sources sheltered by a 501(c)3 tax free status because they can claim a portion of what they do is policy, research and education. Such ads are currently funding some of the most dishonest TV ads that run relentlessly.

Sadly, the Roberts Supreme Court which claims to support state sovereignty compounded the damage caused by the *Citizens United* decision when it also overturned Montana's one hundred year-old law that enforces tight limits on campaign contributions. This model legislation ended an era of wholesale political corruption with two powerful mining companies buying and selling legislators like trading cards. These Supreme Court decisions mean that states as well as the federal government can no longer effectively limit political contributions. When asked at an Internet forum about the *Citizen's United* decision, President Obama recently answered

> "Over the longer term, I think we need to seriously consider mobilizing a constitutional amendment process to overturn Citizens United (assuming the Supreme Court doesn't revisit it)."
>
> "Even if the amendment process falls short," he said, "it can shine a spotlight on the super-PAC phenomenon and help apply pressure for change." I couldn't agree more. For those who believe in political reform, this is an absolutely crucial step to undertake.

Finally, as a woman who fought for causes I believe benefit all families, I feel that electing more women is crucial if we ever hope to create a society based on equality. The 2010 election of Tea Party conservatives that now dominate the House and many state legislatures across the country have undertaken a series of punitive bills that inspired "the war on women" which could never have happened if there were more women in elective positions. For instance:

—The Wisconsin legislature passed and Governor Scott Walker signed into law a bill that repealed long standing legislation guaranteeing equal pay for women.

—South Dakota Republicans in February of 2012 proposed a bill which passed out of committee to make it legal to murder a physician who provides abortion care. Under this bill such a murder would be designated "justifiable homicide." The bill itself has not passed but it may well encourage some fanatic to murder physicians who perform abortions.

—In Maryland, Republicans cut all funds that enable low income children to attend preschool because they argue that women should be at home with their children.

—Arizona now bans all abortions after twenty weeks even if the life or health of the mother in danger.

—Colorado now has a law that denies female employees birth control coverage.

—Virginia pared down their vaginal probe ultra sound bill only because women converged on the capitol to revolt against the bill.

At the national level it is not an overstatement to speak of a "war on women" when access to contraception is being challenged in Congress, and a young woman activist can be called a "slut" by syndicated radio host Rush Limbaugh because she takes a position in favor of health insurance providing contraceptives to students. One may disagree with her position on this issue but the attempts to intimidate women from expressing their views is unacceptable in a civil society. If there is no war on women as some Republicans claim why did the Republican House members take funds out of the health care bill that were set aside for women's programs and transfer these funds to make sure interest rates didn't double on student loans? Why did Republican Presidential candidate and one-term moderate Massachusetts Governor, Mitt Romney, feel it necessary to say he will cut off all funding for Planned Parenthood which is the leading provider of women's health care for poor women? Whatever your stance on these issues, the fact is these decisions were made by male political leaders without enough female voices around them to challenge their misguided actions.

When I arrived in the Illinois state Senate in January, 1997, there were four female Democratic Senators other than myself. Senator Margaret Smith who took over for her husband when he passed away, Earlean Collins, Penny Severns (who died of cancer in 1999) and Evelyn Bowles. It was difficult for me until a couple of years later when Senators Lisa Madigan and Kim Lightford joined our caucus. There has been substantial improvement in the representation of women in the Illinois General Assembly since then including leadership positions that I and other female members worked to attain.

But how sad that in 2010 not only did I lose my seat in Congress, ten out of the eleven Democratic women who won in 2008, lost in 2010. The amount of women serving in congress in 2011 was less than in the 1970s. We cannot afford to lose these voices in the political process. It is important to our society at large that women prepare themselves to do what is necessary to make sure our political institutions, businesses and civic organizations are committed to fairness and equality. For my own part, I will be working closely with groups that are committed to these goals in the years ahead.

In my research for this book I have collected stories and information of a magnitude too large for this book. It is my hope that in the very near future I will be developing an E-Book that I will be giving away to those who sign up and leave their email. That website is: www.playingballwiththebigboys.com

So don't ever forget:

There is more to do to get our country on track, but I believe that Eleanor Roosevelt said it best "the future belongs to those who believe in the beauty of their dreams."

Order Form

email orders: www.playingballwiththebigboys.com

fax orders:708-672-0144

Postal orders: Solutions Unlimited Publishing, 317 E. 11th Street, Chicago Heights, IL 60411,

Please send the following books, discs or reports. I understand that I may return any of them if for any reason they are not what I ordered.

Please send me more FREE information on

_other books, _speaking/seminars, _mailing lists, _consulting

Name: ____________________

Address: ____________________

City: __________ State: __________ Zip: __________

Telephone: ____________________

Email address: ____________________

Book: Playing Ball With The Big Boys $19.95

Sales tax: please add 7 percent

Shipping and Handling: add $6 for the first book, and $4 for each additional book

Payment:(check one)_ check_ credit card_ visa_ MasterCard_ Discover_ _

Card Number_ _ _ _ _ _ _ _ code on back_ _

Name on the Card_ _ _ _ _ _ Exp. Date._ _ /_ _

see: www.playingballwiththebigboys.com